Foc...

Early Childhood

A Handbook for Teachers

by Sharon Ellard

Gospel Publishing House
Springfield, Missouri
02–0404

2nd Printing 2001

Library of Congress Catalog Card Number 93-078159
International Standard Book Number 0-88243-404-7
Printed in the United States of America

Contents

There's more than one way to read a book.

Welcome to <u>Focus on Early Childhood</u>. *This handbook was written to help you plan and teach Bible lessons to young children. Depending on what you want to learn, you may or may not start reading this book from its beginning. Following are a few ways to tailor this handbook to your needs.*

If you are an experienced teacher, you may decide to go straight to a chapter of immediate interest to you. Perhaps you want to learn more about storytelling. Then you could scan the table of contents for a chapter that deals with that topic. Rather than beginning with page 1, you might start at chapter 11, "Telling Techniques—Storytelling." After using helpful parts of that chapter, you could look for another method or idea you want to add to your existing teaching skills.

If you are a brand new teacher, you may want to combine several reading strategies. To gain an overview of its contents, scan the table of contents then flip through the book. As you skim, you may stop to read short portions that deal with challenges you face in your class. Also mark longer sections you want to read soon. You might mark the age-level traits in chapter 4, for example. Eventually, you will want to read this whole book, so try to keep it with your teacher guide. When you begin to prepare a weekly Bible lesson, you can take a few minutes to read a little more from the handbook.

If your church is growing, you may decide to begin with chapters 7 through 10. These chapters describe options for organizing early childhood ministries in churches of various sizes.

Ask the Holy Spirit to guide your reading. The Holy Spirit knows every preschooler in your church. He can combine your abilities and the ideas in this book to build faith in young lives.

It's Not Just Baby-Sitting Anymore

1

Joseph and Mary took him [Baby Jesus] to Jerusalem to present him to the Lord (Luke 2:21).

Question To Answer:

1. *How influential are early childhood Sunday School experiences in the lifelong spiritual development?*

During a modern baby dedication, young parents bring their baby to church to commit themselves to raise their infant in ways that will lead the child to a saving knowledge of Jesus Christ. Often during the same service, the pastor and church also make a commitment to God and the parents, vowing to nurture the child at church so he will come to love and obey God.

Even after making such a dedication, however, churches sometimes fail to understand how experiences in the church nursery and in early childhood Sunday school classes affect spiritual growth. Too often early childhood teachers are viewed as baby-sitters who care for children so parents can worship or attend adult Sunday school. Underestimating the effect of early childhood limits the long-lasting spiritual development that can be nurtured in the first 5 years of life.

LONG-LASTING MINISTRY TO LITTLE ONES

When ministry opportunities are listed, somehow being an adult teacher often seems to be considered a more influential ministry than being a preschool teacher. Yet we all know that Scripture points to the significance of spiritual lessons learned in childhood. In Proverbs God says, "Train a child in the way he should go, and when he is old he will not turn from it" (Proverbs 22:6).

Young children are impressionable. They believe what grown-ups tell them. Young children are forming attitudes that will guide them throughout grade school, throughout high school, and throughout their adult lives. What are these far reaching attitudes? Hopefully, young children who are influenced by Christian teachers will form positive biblical attitudes. "I *love* to come to God's house." "I *like* the way God made me!" "I'm *glad* that God loves me all the time." "I *trust* God to help me." "I *want* to please God." (We'll look closer at developing attitudes and learning early spiritual lessons in chapters 2 and 3.)

Modern education programs like Head Start are set up on the same premise. Educators know they have a much better chance of shaping academic and social attitudes if they begin with preschoolers.

Even so, some Christians still consider teaching in the baby nursery or in preschool classes to be baby-sitting. (Ever heard that comment?) Informed early childhood teachers know, however, that loving relationships and enjoyable Bible learning, at home and in church, form the roots of love, trust, and obedience—three foundations of Christian faith. Perhaps the wrong idea that early childhood ministry is baby-sitting comes from our lack of early childhood memories. Most of us remember very little about our preschool years. Because we lack memories, we may conclude our early years of life lacked lasting importance. Not so. In the absence of personal early memories, we can gain insights from recent research studies that point to the long-term effects of early childhood events.

In Syracuse, New York, a team of early childhood educators provided 108 poor, inner-city, single-parent families with early childhood education and parenting support. As each child entered the first grade, he left the study. No further contact was made with the families until 10 years later when the children were 15 years old. The long-term impact of the early childhood education showed up most impressively in the children's juvenile delinquency rate. In the control group of children who had not received early childhood intervention 22% had criminal records. Only 6% of the children who received early childhood support had delinquency records at all. Court and probation costs were $107,000 for the control group, compared to $12,000 for the children who received early childhood help.

The Syracuse study is significant for early childhood Christian education. The longest lasting effects of the early childhood help in Syracuse showed up in the form of moral choices teenagers made—whether to obey the laws of our society or to break them. Early childhood church workers can help develop biblical morals in preschoolers. Those morals will continue to guide them as Christian teenagers, when they will be faced with life-changing choices about friends, drugs, sex, and careers.

Another research study shows the impact of early experiences on adult behavior. A 30-year study of 698 infants in Hawaii concluded that babies who are consistently loved, cared for, and accepted in the first year of life can thrive even when they face poverty, family breakups, and other handicaps during the rest of their childhood. One-third of the children studied in Hawaii grew up in these kinds of adverse conditions. Even so, 25% of these children grew into competent, confident adults. The researchers found themselves wondering why most of the children in these kinds of homes developed problems while a few seemed to thrive in spite of the handicaps. According to the study, each of the resilient adults had benefited from at least one devoted caregiver—a parent, a grandparent, or a sibling—*during the first year of life.* This early caregiving had helped to develop positive attitudes in the children that remained with them throughout childhood, adolescence, and young adult life.

EARLY SPIRITUAL LESSONS

Such research findings lead us back to the principle of Proverbs 22: "Train a child in the way he should go, and when he is old he will not turn from it." That verse should be a motto not only for parents of preschoolers but also for all Christian early childhood teachers as we devote ourselves to early Christian education. As parents place their young children in our keeping, we do want to provide safe, physical care for each child. But by remembering that early childhood Christian education is not just baby-sitting anymore, we can also look beyond giving physical care to laying spiritual foundations for babies, toddlers, and preschoolers.

As we come to think of ourselves as more than baby-sitters, we ask the Holy Spirit to guide our interaction with children. We watch for moments of wonder to pray with children. We equip our rooms with pictures, posters, tapes, books, and toys to teach about God. We give individual attention to children.

To give attention to children is one of the best means of beginning to influence them. Jesus set an example of how to show this kind of faith-building attention. He took time out from talking about adult issues, like settling disputes among believers and teaching how God views marriage (see Matthew 18 and 19), to invite children up onto His lap to bless them (Matthew 19:14). Jesus' disciples viewed little children as interruptions in Jesus' ministry to adults. But Jesus gave importance to ministering to children.

Ministry Check:

The Holy Spirit is your partner in Christian education. Pause right now and ask the Holy Spirit to guide your teaching and to cause your ministry to young children to influence them to love, trust, and obey God for a lifetime.

How Does Faith Begin To Grow? 2

All the days planned for me were written in your book before I was one day old (Psalm 139:16, *International Children's Bible*).

Questions To Answer:

1. What early events lead children to love God?

2. How do relationships with Christian teachers and parents affect children's faith?

3. What can Christian teachers do to promote the development of love, trust, and obedience in preschoolers?

It was 1:15 a.m. I was wide awake—and glad to be. Our daughter had just been born. Nurses huddled around her—giving her shots, putting drops in her eyes, pricking her foot for blood tests. She was not happy. But we were. After 9 months (and 10 days) of waiting and praying, we were seeing our daughter for the first time. Even with her eyes puffy and squeezed shut as she squalled with displeasure, she looked beautiful to us. That was the physical birth of our child.

When the nurses finished their testing, they wrapped Barbara in a blanket and brought her to us. I began to soothe her softly. "It's OK, little one. It's OK." Her crying lessened, and she turned her head toward my voice for the first look at her mother. That response began our daughter's first spiritual lesson—

responding to love.

In the days that followed, my husband and I continued the process of preparing our daughter for her salvation that would come years later. Even from that first moment, though, when we spoke to our newborn daughter and she responded, we began the birthing of faith in her life.

WHAT IS FAITH?

In talking about early spiritual development, we will define faith as "heartfelt attitudes of trust and love in God that result in obedience to Him."

The birth of faith is essential to spiritual growth. Hebrews 11:6 states clearly, "Without faith no one can please God. Anyone who comes to God must believe that he is real and that he rewards those who truly want to find him" (*International Children's Bible*).

Just as a newborn looks very different from the toddler he will be 12 months later and from the high school graduate he will be 17 years after that, the birth of faith in a preschooler looks different from the mature faith of an adult believer. Babies and toddlers first develop faith in parents and Christian teachers. Loving, trusting, and wanting to obey people who love us are the first steps toward loving, trusting, and wanting to obey God. First John talks about this path to faith, "Anyone who does not love his brother, whom he has seen, cannot love God, whom he has not seen" (1 John 4:20). Children who come to love people they can see will find it easier to love God whom they can't see.

WHEN DOES FAITH BEGIN TO GROW?

In Psalm 139 David expresses his confidence that God began to shape his spiritual life even before birth. "All the days planned for me were written in your book *before I was one day old*" (Psalm 139:16, *International Children's Bible*, emphasis added).

In God's book, life begins before birth. God's plans for each of us are complete before our birth. God knows who will influence us. He knows how well we will be loved, how well we will be taught. God knows what choices we will make. He knows all this before we take our first breath.

As Christian teachers of young children, we want our students to begin to develop strong faith in God. We want the children to want to love, to trust, and to obey God. What lessons, what relationships, will help children's faith grow?

BIBLE STORIES NURTURE FAITH

In Psalm 78 God instructs His people to tell children about the great miracles of God. God says to tell children about God's power over Pharaoh. Describe God's escape route through the Red Sea. Rehearse the crash of the walls of Jericho. What is the purpose of telling stories about the mighty acts of God? According to Psalm 78:

> The Lord…gave the teachings to Israel. And he commanded our ancestors to teach them to their children. Then their children would know them, even their children not yet born. And they would tell their children. *So they would all trust God.* They would not forget what God had done. Instead, *they would obey his commands* (Psalm 78:5–7, *International Children's Bible*, emphasis added).

Romans 10:17 also tells how teaching God's Word affects the development of faith. "Faith cometh by hearing, and hearing by the word of God" (KJV). Children who grow up hearing Bible stories about the power of God will have seeds of faith planted in their minds and hearts. Early childhood Christian education focuses on nurturing faith through teaching how God helped His people in Bible times. Bible stories form the core of early childhood Christian education.

The Bible is a historic record of God's dealings with His people. God tells the good, the bad, and the ugly. One responsibility of early childhood teachers is to carefully choose age-appropriate Bible stories to tell young children. Just as a parent would offer strained applesauce to an infant rather than a whole apple, Christian teachers offer God's Word to children in portions and in forms children can understand and thrive on. Chapter 11 will describe good ways to teach Bible stories so young children come to love hearing God's Word.

GOOD MODELS NURTURE FAITH

As Christian teachers, most of us understand the impact Bible stories can have on faith development. How well do we understand, however, the impact our personal examples have on children's spiritual development?

Watch preschoolers play house. Listen to what they say. The children will talk to one another and to their dolls with the same words and in the same tones that their parents and teachers have used with them. The life-styles of grown-ups affect spiritual development because children learn by imitating.

In Ephesians 5:1,2, Christians are told to imitate God, their Heavenly Father. Parents and Christian teachers who imitate God show young children what God is like and give the children a pattern to imitate.

BEING LOVED NURTURES FAITH

David's faith in God was based on his relationship with God: David **felt loved** by God so David loved God. Being loved helps a child learn to love.

God designs newborns to thrive on their parents' love. Modern research allow us a glimpse of God's design of the human infant. Consider several facts we now know about infants.

- ■ For several weeks while a child develops in the womb, 250,000 brain cells develop every minute.
- ■ At birth a child's brain is equipped with trillions of neurons to record interactions with parents.
- ■ From the moment of birth, a newborn will turn his head in the direction of his mother's voice. (The baby has been able to hear her voice from the sixth month after conception.)

■ From birth newborns focus best on objects 8 to 11 inches from their eyes. That is just the distance between an infant's face and their parent's face when a parent holds the baby in the crook of his arm.

■ From birth children show a strong preference for gazing at the human face over any other kind of picture.

Is all of this coincidence? I believe these traits come from God's design. He has designed babies to focus on their parents' faces—faces that will show their first close look at expressions of love. Parents who show love for infants by gentle touches, loving facial expressions, and soft coos and words, begin building bonds of love. Feeling loved by parents and teachers as a baby, a toddler, and a preschooler sets the stage for feeling loved by God.

CHURCH TEACHERS CAN NURTURE FAITH

At church, Christian teachers who understand God's design of infants, toddlers, and preschoolers can respond to that design in ways that will help faith grow. Remember, we are defining **faith** as "heartfelt attitudes of **love** and **trust** in God that result in **obedience** to Him." Christian teachers can affect spiritual growth in important ways.

As you rock babies, comfort toddlers, and play with preschoolers, have you thought of yourself as nurturing faith? If you believe that what you do in the nursery will make a difference in the spiritual lives of the children, then you will do the following:

■ You will keep expanding your understanding of the children.

■ You will keep looking for better ways to teach the children.

■ You will ask the Holy Spirit to guide your planning.

■ You will become a minister to young children.

Does that sound out of reach? The information in this handbook is designed to help you teach young children so they will grow spiritually. As you read the rest of this book, ask yourself some questions. "Am I already teaching babies, toddlers, and preschoolers in these ways? Will this kind of teaching lead to the children's feeling loved? Will the children trust me because of the way I teach them? Will their love and trust for me help them want to obey me? Will loving, trusting, and obeying me help the children learn to love, trust, and obey God?"

Ministry Check:

On a piece of paper write the words trust, love, obedience, faith. Under each word write two ways you are encouraging the growth of these attitudes in the lives of young children while you teach them at church.

What Do Children Need To Know Before First Grade?

3

> All Scripture is given by God and is useful for teaching and for showing people what is wrong in their lives. It is useful for correcting faults and teaching how to live right (2 Timothy 3:16, *International Children's Bible*).

Questions To Answer:

1. What spiritual lessons can preschoolers learn?

2. How can Christian education change the lives of preschoolers?

For most children in the USA, formal education begins in kindergarten. But children who will do well in school have already learned many important lessons before their first day of formal schooling. Robert Fulghum describes this early learning in *All I Really Need To Know I Learned in Kindergarten.* [1]

> All I really need to know about how to live and what to do and how to be I learned in kindergarten. Wisdom was not at the top of the graduate-school mountain, but there in the sandpile at Sunday School. These are the things I learned. Share everything. Play fair. Don't hit people. Put things back where you found them. Clean up your own mess. Don't take things that aren't yours. Say you're sorry when you hurt somebody...Everything you need to know is there somewhere. The Golden Rule and love and basic sanitation. Ecology and politics and equality and sane living. Take any

one of those items and extrapolate it into sophisticated adult terms and apply it to your family or your work or your government or our world and it holds true and clear and firm. (Used by permission.)

Fulghum's lessons parallel an even more important kind of lessons preschoolers can learn—Bible lessons.

GOD'S PHILOSOPHY OF EDUCATION

Deuteronomy describes God's philosophy of how to organize Christian education.

Love the Lord your God with all your heart, soul and strength. Always remember these commands I give you today. *Teach them to your children.* Talk about them when you *sit at home* and *walk along the road.* Talk about them when you *lie down* and when you *get up* (Deuteronomy 6:5–7, *International Children's Bible*, emphasis added).

Let's note several points about God's philosophy of early Christian education.

1. God wants children to love Him.

Obedience follows love. Early Bible lessons should influence children to love God.

2. God wants parents to teach children.

In God's Word the primary responsibility for early spiritual training rests with parents. The church should support parents in Christian education.

3. God wants children to learn spiritual lessons during everyday routines.

In terms of today's routines God wants parents to talk about His commands in the car, at the grocery store, during meals, at bedtime, at the zoo, and at any other times when children and parents are together. Christian education at church can imitate on-the-go-learning by including as many hands-on learning activities as possible in Bible lessons.

4. God wants children to respond to Him in all parts of their lives.

Christian education can help children become aware of God's presence and love whether they are praying or playing, in Sunday school or in day care, at church or at home.

In God's philosophy, Christian education prepares children to live by biblical patterns 7 days a week, 24 hours a day.

EDUCATING THE WHOLE PERSON

Look back at the first part of the Deuteronomy passage. Verse 5 describes God's desire that we love Him with our whole being—with all our heart, our soul, and our strength. In the New Testament Jesus added one more area. "Love the Lord your God with all your **heart** and with all your **soul** and with all your **mind** and with all your **strength**" (Mark 12:30). Christian education that teaches children to obey that commandment involves changing the students':

> Minds .... Knowledge
> Hearts .... Attitudes
> Strengths .... Abilities and actions
> Souls .... Spiritual response to teaching

Bible lessons that involve only the mind, for example, neglect attitudes, abilities, actions, and spirit.

Knowledge—Education of the Mind

The education of the mind is an important part of Christian education. John 4:23 says that God wants to be worshipped in "spirit and in truth" (KJV). Bible knowledge allows children to learn truth about God. Teaching knowledge goals involves familiar Bible learning activities.

1. Learning Bible words. Even babies and toddlers can begin to connect words such as *Bible*, *church*, and *Jesus* with pictures and objects they see at church and at home.

2. Memorizing Bible verses. Many preschoolers can memorize quickly. To qualify as true knowledge, however, children need to understand the meaning of the verses they memorize.

3. Hearing Bible stories. To remember and understand Bible stories, preschoolers need to see lots of pictures as they listen to the stories. The younger the child, the fewer words he will understand and the more pictures he will need.

4. Asking questions. In some early childhood classes, children ask more questions than teachers do. When the child asks a question, he presents a teachable moment.

When children achieve knowledge goals, they will know what is right in God's eyes. The goal of Christian education, however, doesn't stop with knowledge.

Attitudes—Education of the Heart

Psalm 119:11 says, "Thy word have I hid in mine *heart*" (KJV). The psalmist could have said *mind*. But learning God's Word went beyond rote memorization for the psalmist. He learned God's Word with his mind *and wanted* to obey God's Word with his *heart*. Bible learning affected his attitudes as well as his mind. How can Christian teachers help Bible knowledge get into students' hearts as well as into their minds?

1. Use music to teach. Even young babies respond to the emotion of music by waving their arms in time with the rhythm. Music appeals to both sides of the brain. The words lodge in the logical part of the mind. The tunes and rhythms affect the emotional side of the brain.

2. Let children make choices. Plan lessons so children get to choose some learning activities. When a child chooses an activity, his learning experiences will affect his feelings as well as his intellect.

3. Help children succeed. Plan learning activities at which all children will succeed. By succeeding, children build confidence in their ability to learn.

4. Always build up the child. "Encourage one another and build each other up" (1 Thessalonians 5:11). God wants Christian growth to be marked by encouragement at all ages. If you praise a child's efforts to learn, he will want to continue to use what he learns in daily living.

Bible lessons that include these elements teach children to enjoy church, resulting in an attitude the psalmist shared: "I was **happy** when they said to me, 'Let's go to the Temple of the Lord'" (Psalm 122:1, *International Children's Bible*).

Abilities—Education of the Body

Ability objectives help children become doers of God's Word. "**Do** what God's teaching says; do not just listen and do nothing" (James 1:22, *International Children's Bible*). Christian teachers can plan ways to let children practice doing what the Bible says.

1. Use hands-on learning activities. Learning is a product of doing. When babies learn to walk, they practice. They step around furniture. They hold on to parents' hands. They push walkers around the rooms. After months of practice, they are ready to take their first wobbly steps without holding on. The same principle applies to spiritual skills.

2. Plan for play with purpose. Teachers who play with children at church can use their own actions and conversations to connect play with Bible lessons. Play with purpose allows children to put into practice ideas they have heard the teacher talk about. Children who use play at church to practice what the Bible says are much more likely to obey the Bible during the week than children who only hear Bible lessons at church.

3. Emphasize Christlike behavior. When Christ lived on earth, His life showed how God deals with us. Christian teachers can show their students what God is like too. Preschool children learn through imitating the words and actions of people around them. So, if you want children to take turns, plan ways to take turns with the children during Bible lessons. Draw attention to the way you take turns. Help children enjoy taking turns at church. Praise children when you notice them taking turns. Tell the children God is pleased when He sees us take turns. Soon preschoolers will begin to imitate Christlike behavior.

4. Love the children. Remember Ephesians 5:1,2. The children will imitate God if they love God. The first step to loving and imitating God is loving and imitating Christian teachers and parents.

Actions—Education for Living

Most people know more than they put into practice in their lives. Sunday school will have little effect in the lives of young children unless the children can transfer what they learn at church on Sunday to what they live at home Monday through Saturday. The practice of play with purpose helps children make that transfer, but early childhood teachers can increase the frequency of applying lessons to lives in other ways too.

1. Tell life application stories. For today's children, parts of Bible stories may seem odd. Today's child, for example, gets water from a faucet, not a well. They travel in vehicles, not on animals. Life application stories bring the principles of Bible stories into modern times, so modern children can understand how to live the lesson in today's world.

2. Act out Bible events. Drama brings principles to action. Many preschoolers enjoy acting out a story their teacher describes. Drama lets children become active in the story. That activity may transfer to everyday actions during the week.

3. Plan to remind the children of Bible principles. Children learn through repetition. Expect to remind children many, many, many times of what God wants before the children begin to remember on their own.

4. Send home reminders of the Bible lesson. Keep in mind, God gives parents the primary responsibility for teaching their children to live for God. Support parents' role as teachers. Send home games, crafts, placemats, charts, etc., that encourage the children to continue the lesson during the week—to put the lesson into action. Then pray that the Holy Spirit will remind parents to teach spiritual lessons during the week.

SEVEN GOALS OF CHRISTIAN EDUCATION

Balanced, life-changing Bible learning includes seven goals. These goals can be learned by people from 1 to 92. At different ages different goals become prominent, but Christian education at all age-levels should keep these goals in focus. These are the seven general goals of Christian Education. During early childhood we are laying foundations. By beginning toward spiritual goals in the early years, we not only prepare children to live for God as preschoolers, but we also equip children with basics that they can build on as they grow.

As Christian teachers, we need to know what young children can learn. So let's look at examples of how the seven goals of Christian education relate to preschoolers' knowledge, attitudes, abilities, and actions. By the time each child is ready to start first grade, he should have reached the following goals.

Goal 1—Salvation

During early childhood, we want to prepare each preschool child for the experience of spiritual new birth. Much of what we do in early childhood education will be pre-evangelism. Pre-evangelism lessons prepare children for the time when the Holy Spirit will draw them to salvation.

Knowledge

- Each child should know that God loves him all the time—even when he's bad.
- Each child should understand that Jesus lived on earth and that He died to forgive our sins.

Attitudes

- Each child should love God and His Son Jesus.
- Each child should desire to please God by doing what the Bible says.

Abilities

- Each child should feel comfortable talking to God in a number of ways.

Actions

- Each child should be able to express love for God in prayer, in song, and in living.

■ Each child should begin to acknowledge mistakes and wrongdoing.

Goal 2—Biblical Knowledge

Children's response to Bible knowledge should affect their attitudes and actions as well as their intellect.

Knowledge

■ Each child should know the Bible is more important than any other book.

■ Each child should know that the Bible is God's way of telling us how to live.

Attitudes

■ Each child should enjoy hearing Bible stories.

■ Each child should want to do what the Bible teaches.

Abilities

■ Each child should be able to retell Bible stories and quote simple Bible verses.

■ Each child should be able to apply some biblical truths to everyday living.

Actions

■ Each child should handle the Bible reverently.

■ Each child should begin to base his actions on what the Bible says.

Goal 3—A Spirit-Filled Life

The Holy Spirit is at work in the lives of preschoolers. Children will become more aware of the Holy Spirit as they grow older. In early childhood, children can develop an important attitude toward God's Spirit.

Attitude

■ Each child should develop sensitivity to spiritual events and be receptive to the Holy Spirit.

Goal 4—Christian Growth

Preschoolers can develop character traits that are foundations of later Christian growth.

Knowledge

■ Each child should know the Bible teaches how to live like Jesus.

Attitudes

■ Each child should want to be like Jesus.

■ Each child should enjoy worship experiences.

Abilities

■ Each child should begin to understand how to react to problems and disappointments in a Christlike way.

Actions

■ Each child should begin to experience times of worship.

■ Each child should begin to follow Jesus' example of living.

Goal 5—Personal Commitment

As each child becomes aware that God made him and that God loves him, he will begin to feel that he has an important part in God's plans. Under the ministry of the Holy Spirit, such children will respond by committing their lives to God.

Knowledge

■ Each child should know God made him for a good purpose.

■ Each child should know Jesus is his Friend.

■ Each child should know Sunday is God's special day and church is God's special house.

Attitudes

- Each child should appreciate the world God made.
- Each child should be happy with the way God made him.
- Each child should feel secure in God's love.

Abilities

- Each child should begin to develop God-given abilities.

Actions

- Each child should joyfully attend God's house and participate in its activities.

Goal 6—Christian Service

Preschoolers can begin to express love for God in service. They can begin to serve God and others and to feel a part of the Church.

Knowledge

- Each child should think of church as a place where we worship God and learn how God wants us to help others.
- Each child should know everyone is welcome at church.
- Each child should know that people in other countries need to hear about Jesus.

Attitudes

- Each child should want to please God by helping others.
- Each child should appreciate Jesus because He helped others.
- Each child should want others to know Jesus.

Abilities

- Each child should develop abilities to use in serving God and others.

Actions

■ Each child should begin to tell friends about Jesus.

Goal 7—Christian Living

Preschoolers can form living habits and patterns that help them apply Christian principles to every part of life.

Knowledge

■ Each child should know there are right and wrong ways to act.

■ Each child should know that God will help him do right.

■ Each child should understand that his actions can affect others.

■ Each child should begin to understand that others have equal rights with him.

Attitudes

■ Each child should want to please God.

Abilities

■ Each child should begin to choose to do right.

■ Each child should begin to show love to others.

Actions

■ Each child should perform simple tasks.

■ Each child should continue to develop self-control.

What do children need to know before first grade? A lot! Christian teachers play an important part of teaching preschoolers early lessons that will help them love, trust, and obey God from crib to grave.

Ministry Check:

Check how well you plan Bible lessons to teach the whole child—mind, heart, body, and spirit.

Knowledge

__ I use Bible words (*Jesus, God, church, Bible*) in the lessons.

__ I plan ways the children can repeat Bible words in lessons.

__ I teach Bible verses in interesting ways.

__ I make sure children understand Bible verses they learn.

Attitudes

__ I use music to get children's attention and to teach.

__ I plan lessons so children can choose between good learning activities at least sometimes.

__ I help children succeed at Bible lesson activities.

Abilities

__ I plan hands-on learning activities that let children practice Bible learning at church.

__ I use conversation to connect play activities with Bible ideas children are learning.

Actions

__ I tell life application stories so children hear an example of how to live the Bible lesson at home.

__ I use drama to allow children to act out ways to use Bible lessons in everyday life.

__ I send home reminders about Bible lessons with children so parents can continue Bible learning during the week.

[1] Robert Fulghum, *All I Really Need To Know I Learned in Kindergarten* (New York, NY: Villard Books, a division of Random House, Inc., 1989. Used by permission.)

God Didn't Goof When He Made Preschoolers

4

When I was a child, I talked like a child; I
thought like a child; I made plans like a child
(1 Corinthians 13:11, *International Children's
Bible*).

Questions To Answer:

1. *What are common traits of preschool children?*

2. *How do the normal traits of preschoolers affect the way we teach them the Bible?*

God designs young children to learn Bible lessons in childlike ways. When Jesus invited the children to come, He took them up into His arms. Let's think about that scene. Imagine one child sitting in Jesus' lap while another struggles to climb up too. Do the children touch Jesus' face? Does a 2-year-old show Jesus a rock he found? When the children leave, does Jesus have a dusty footprint on His robe?

Jesus responded to children in a way that was right for their age. Jesus would never have held one of His fisherman disciples on His lap. The idea would be ridiculous and all wrong. But Jesus *did* hold little children as He blessed them. He accepted children who came with wiggles, giggles, and dirty hands.

As teachers of preschoolers, we need to learn what kind of teaching fits our young students. Just as we wouldn't expect students in the adult class to sing action songs, we shouldn't expect students in the preschool class to sit still throughout a Bible lesson. Just as we wouldn't ask adult students to sit on the floor and build with blocks in Sunday school, we shouldn't furnish preschool church classes with nothing but tables and chairs. All students, whatever their ages, learn better when their lessons and classrooms are designed to fit their learning styles. Since we teach eternal lessons about God and the Bible, matching teaching styles to learning styles becomes even more important.

COMMON PRESCHOOL TRAITS

Preschoolers, from age 1 through kindergarten, have some traits in common. All preschoolers, for example, are active. Even though they often hear the phrase, "Sit still," their bodies are not able to put those words into practice for long. It's important to know what is normal behavior for young children. The chart in this chapter lists a few of the most common early childhood traits. The left column of the chart lists normal preschool traits. The right column suggests one or more ways a Christian teacher can plan Bible lessons to match Bible lessons with early childhood learning styles.

PRESCHOOL TRAITS	TEACHER'S RESPONSE IN LESSONS
Physical	
Active	Plan learning activities that involve movement.
Uncoordinated fingers	For older preschoolers plan very simple cutting and/or gluing activities. Expect to teach the how-tos of gluing and cutting. Praise all efforts.

Acquire new skills	Plan learning activities that use children's new skills, like drawing, climbing, coloring, jumping, etc. Preschoolers are enthusiastic about their new skills. By connecting Bible learning with these skills, pre-schoolers become enthusiastic about Bible learning too.
Mental	
Think literally	Teach Bible lessons with concrete objects such as blocks, dolls, toy cars, etc. Use abstract ideas sparingly.
Short attention spans	Plan a number of short activities for each lesson. Adjust the time spent on each activity according to the age of the child and the interest in the activity.
Limited vocabulary	Use simple words and short sentences. Add church words to children's vocabulary—Jesus, Bible, prayer, etc. Rephrase adult ideas into words little ones know. Be alert to preschoolers who parrot words without understanding what they mean. Help them understand.
Forget easily	Be prepared to calmly remind children of rules many times. Understand when children forget a lesson from a previous week.

Benefit from repetition	Repeat an activity as long as children are interested. Teach the same lesson objectives in several ways.
Learn by imitating	Take part in all activities with children. Teach by example the lessons you want children to learn—sharing, speaking softly, praying, etc.
Emotional/Social	
Intense feelings	Expect emotional outbursts. Help children express needs with words. Pace the lesson to avoid over-tiring children; preschoolers are more emotional when they are tired or hungry.
Fearful, anxious	Take time to win their confidence. Help tearful children become involved in enjoyable learning activities. Try to keep at least one teacher the same from Sunday to Sunday.
Play alongside others	Use games, dramas, etc., that allow all children to take part at the same time. Provide duplicates of favorite toys so several children can use them at the same time. Many children will begin actually playing with others during preschool or kindergarten.
See life from own perspective	Don't expect children to know how to cooperate. Establish and repeat rituals for taking turns, cooperating, and sharing until rituals become habits.

Need to learn life skills	Allow children to make choices. Offer two options to choose between. ("Do you want to use paint or crayons to color your picture?") Don't use a question if you don't intend to give the children a choice.
Respond to praise	Catch the children doing good and praise that behavior. Your praise will encourage children to repeat the good behavior. When children are learning new skills, your praise will encourage them to keep trying until the skill is mastered.
Need attention	Give children loving attention. Remember, children who don't receive attention for good behavior will use bad behavior to get attention. Your loving attention helps build the faith in God's loving attention.
Spiritual	
Learning to trust	Care for the children as well as teach them. As they receive consistent, loving care from adults, children learn to trust, a vital part of growing faith.
Learning first ideas about God and Jesus	Speak of God and Jesus in happy terms. Create activities around pictures of Jesus. Tell children how much Jesus loves them. Sing happy songs about God and Jesus. Tell them God is pleased when they learn at church. Be sure they feel God loves them all the time.

Forming attitudes about church	Make learning at church a happy experience for children. Express pleasure at seeing each child. Plan learning experiences that children will enjoy.
Worship spontaneously	Provide many moments of wonder about God's creation of the world, babies, family, pets, etc. These will allow children to respond to God from their hearts.

Have you encountered these traits in the children you teach at church? Be assured that such characteristics are normal in preschoolers. As you match your teaching plans to the children's abilities, you and the children will enjoy church more and learn more about God and His ways.

COMMON TRAITS OF INFANTS

Babies come with God-given characteristics too. Teachers who minister in the church nursery help form infants' first ideas about God's house and God's people. At first, ministry in the church nursery is dominated by the physical needs of the babies. Even so, by consistently ministering to the physical needs of the babies, the church nursery teachers help babies begin to trust that they will be well loved and cared for at church.

Ministry in the church nursery goes beyond ministering to physical needs, however. The following chart begins with the physical needs and traits of babies and suggests ways to expand ministry to their mental, social, and spiritual development. The left column lists common traits of babies during the first 12 months of life. The right column suggests some simple ways teachers can nurture babies in the church nursery.

BABY TRAITS	TEACHER'S RESPONSE IN NURSERY
Physical	
Limited body control	Never leave babies unattended on a changing table or any raised surface.
Immobile at first	Change babies' positions from lying on back in crib, to sitting in swing, to lying on stomach on a floor blanket.
Sensitive skin	Check diapers every hour and change as needed. Check with parents before using cremes.
Need frequent nourishment	Use care cards to record babies who nurse or take formula. Feed on demand.
Susceptible to infections	Accept only healthy babies. Create routines for cleaning and disinfecting cribs, changing tables, toys, etc., after each use. Ask adults in the nursery to wash their hands when they arrive, after wiping noses, before feeding babies, and after changing a diaper. Post printed health guidelines in the nursery.
Learning to focus their eyes	Place simple, high-contrast pictures and objects 10 to 15 inches from babies. Use mobiles, laminated pictures, and safe toys. Position such visuals near cribs, diaper-changing stations, swings, etc.

Move from random to intentional movements	Position safe toys where random movement will sometimes bring contact. Eventually the baby will attempt to reach the objects on purpose.
Desire to explore	Provide crawling babies with boxes, tunnels, and cushions to maneuver over, under, and around.

Mental

Learning language	Talk to babies. They will enjoy hearing the sound of your voice. Call all babies by name. "Dialogue" with babies who are cooing—take turns, letting them coo, followed by your talking. Make animal and machine sounds for older babies. Connect sounds with toy animals, pictures, and vehicles. As you care for a baby, describe what you are doing. Enjoy simple Sunday school songs and action rhymes with baby.
Enjoy repetition	Make some learning activities a permanent part of the nursery schedule. Place safe, cleanable toys in containers. Add simple instructions to each container so anyone can teach a Bible idea with the toys. As such activities are repeated, babies will learn.

Learn through senses	Provide variety of safe, colorful toys that can be thoroughly cleaned. Hang an unbreakable mirror where babies can see themselves. Add sound toys and taped praise and worship music. Avoid stuffed toys that can't be laundered.
Unaware of hazards	Cover electrical outlets. Remove unstable equipment. Sand or pad sharp edges. Locate and remove objects small enough to swallow or to lodge in throat.
Emotional/Social	
Quick mood changes	React calmly to cries. Check for cause of distress—hunger, diaper irritation, tiredness, boredom, desire for attention, etc. Distract babies with an interesting toy or sight. Change baby's position or location.
Need attention	Rock and soothe the babies. Give attention when babies are happy as well as when crying. Enjoy holding, playing, and talking with them as much as time allows. Allow your facial expressions to communicate pleasure and understanding to babies. Sing to the babies. Play simple games, such as covering and uncovering a toy with a cloth.

Communicate with body language	Remain sensitive to babies' body language. Give attention that matches the messages the baby sends with gestures and expressions (e.g., when tired, cuddle baby; when alert, offer toys, play simple imitation games, etc.)
Can be over-stimulated	Stay alert to baby's body language. If baby turns face away or becomes fussy, stop that kind of attention. Some babies enjoy having time alone to explore or relax at their own "pace."
Respond to praise	Applaud and smile at babies' achievements. Even very young babies will repeat behavior that received praise.
Fearful of strangers	Try to provide care that is consistent with care baby receives at home. Use care cards to learn home routines. Try to distract a crying baby with toys. Be prepared to call for parent if baby cannot be comforted within 10 to 15 minutes.
Learning to love	Express affection for babies. Stroke, pat, and tickle as appropriate, but always respect a child's desire not to be touched. In a group setting, like a church nursery, it's better to avoid kissing because of the potential of passing infections. Many expressions of affection are welcome.

Enjoy watching	Place babies where they can watch teachers and other babies.
Play alongside peers	Provide duplicates of favorite toys. Watch for safety from babies who don't know how to be gentle. Separate babies as needed to protect them.

Spiritual

Learning basics of relationships	Nurture babies consistently to develop their ability to love and trust others. Later, babies can transfer love and trust to their relationship with God and Jesus.
Discover Jesus	Relate pictures of Jesus to happy feelings. Cuddle babies as you show them simple, colorful Bible picture books and pictures. Create simple games for finding Jesus' picture. Help babies to succeed.
Dependent on parents	Tell parents about babies' good times in the nursery. Send home ideas for Bible activities to do with babies during the week. Distribute or write a newsletter that informs parents about spiritual growth in their little ones.

Children are wonderfully complex, so no list can describe all the traits God gives each child. This chapter highlights some common traits. When teachers respond in ways that match God's design of young children, they are more likely to become Jesus' disciples.

Ministry Check:

Which of the age-level traits listed fit children in your class? Write children's names by traits that match their behavior.

How do you currently respond to these age-level traits as you plan your lesson? as you teach?

Highlight responses in the right column that you want to add to your teaching style.

Learning To Teach The Way Preschoolers Learn 5

Jesus said, "Whoever [receives] welcomes a little child like this in my name [receives] welcomes me" (Matthew 18:5).

Questions To Answer:

1. *What routines match the way preschoolers learn to trust, to love, and to obey God?*

2. *Which routines can I use to help faith grow in the young children of my church?*

NURTURE LOVE, TRUST, & OBEDIENCE

You can nurture spiritual growth in your class. How? By accepting the behavior of preschoolers as being the way God designed them and by establishing teaching routines that match the way children learn. This chapter suggests 10 routines you can use to teach preschoolers to love, to trust, and to obey God. Ask God to help you decide which of the following routines will develop heartfelt love, trust, and obedience in each child you teach. (Chapters 11 and 12 describe some specific early childhood teaching methods.)

1. Look happy to see the children.

If you express pleasure when each child arrives at church, the children will come to feel that you love them. You might say something such as, "Hi, Lucas. I was hoping you'd be at church today." If you look forward to seeing the children, they will look forward to seeing you. Young children who feel their teachers' gladness to see them at church will come to think God is happy to see them too.

2. Help the preschoolers "settle in" to the classroom.

Most young children prefer to be with their parents. God has designed them that way. Sunday school teachers show love for babies, toddlers, and preschoolers by planning ways to ease the transition from being with parents to being in church. So make your room inviting. Play soothing worship music as babies and toddlers arrive. Begin teaching when the first child arrives. Engage new arrivals with interesting sights or toys. Babies may enjoy watching a mobile turn, playing with a busy box, or seeing themselves in a mirror. Toddlers usually enjoy playing with pop-up toys, riding toys, or stacking toys. Preschoolers like to watch a hamster, play with maze beads, or cut play dough shapes. (Remember to use conversation to relate each activity to the Bible lesson.) Soon the children will begin to look forward to interesting activities at church; they will eventually clap and smile when they arrive at church. This kind of body language encourages parents to attend church more faithfully. Then, the babies, toddlers, and preschoolers begin to establish the routine of coming to God's house and learning God's ways.

3. Provide a variety of learning activities in each lesson.

Preschoolers have short attention spans. To teach young children effectively, you will need to prepare a number of short activities that reinforce the same lesson. Every time you change to another activity, you will draw the children's attention back to the lesson. *Sesame Street* uses this approach. At the end of each fast-paced program, a character says, "This program was brought to you by the letter B and the number 8." Before class prepare a variety of active and quiet activities from the teacher's quarterly and your own ideas. Be sure each activity teaches a part of the lesson. During Sunday school decide how much time to spend on each activity depending on student response. As you practice this approach to teaching young children, you will gradually become confident in pacing each Bible lesson.

4. Respond quickly and gently to the physical needs of babies, toddlers, and preschoolers.

Physical needs dominate in early childhood ministries. A baby or young child will not be able to focus on teaching if he is feeling hungry or hot, sleepy or grumpy. Help children identify their needs. To a tired child you might say, "Juan, come here and rest on the cushions with me. I want to show you some pictures of things God made."

When teachers are sympathetic with and care for children's physical needs, children begin to trust their teachers to take care of them. Such teachers are setting the stage for children's learning to trust that God understands their needs too and will also take care of them. So when possible, be prepared to change a lesson in response to a child's needs. When a baby turns his face from the picture you show him, for example, accept that signal. Remove the picture and change activities. He may be ready to eat. He may want time alone. He may respond to cuddling.

As preschoolers mature, their physical needs become less pressing. If you teach kindergarten children, you will probably spend less time ministering to physical needs. But all the way through early childhood, try to learn the habits of the babies, toddlers, and preschoolers you teach, so you will be able to build their trust by responding to needs.

5. Plan time each week to put the lesson into practice.

James 1:22 says, "Do what God's teaching says; do not just listen and do nothing" (*International Children's Bible*). Practice time at church allows children to go beyond just *hearing* the lesson to begin *doing* (obeying) the lesson. When children can practice the lesson at church, teachers are present to *guide* the children's first attempts to do what the Bible says. For young children, practice usually takes the form of play. How do children practice walking, talking, being friends, and so on? They practice through play. Use "play with purpose" to connect the Bible story the children heard with the everyday living they do when outside the church building. You might build a Lego road and vehicle, for example, and pretend to give rides to people who want to come to church.

6. Participate in activities with the children.

This principle has already been mentioned several times in this handbook, and it will be repeated again. It is probably one of the most important principles in teaching preschoolers. By your example, you can show babies, toddlers, and preschoolers how to share, take turns, cooperate, be kind—obey God. When children fuss over a ball, you can show them how to roll or bounce the ball back and forth. Rather than letting children push each other on the slide, you can stand nearby and say, "Now it's Stephi's turn. Jordan will have a turn next."

As children come to count on you to be fair, they will begin to wait more patiently for their own turn. They will come to trust you to give each of them a turn. These kinds of play rituals allow even babies and toddlers to begin to put principles of Christian living into practice.

By the time they celebrate their sixth birthday, children can have a pretty good start at sharing, taking turns, and cooperating IF adults have shown them *how* on a consistent basis. These kinds of experiences prepare children to want to obey God, because they trust God to protect them and provide for them just as their teachers do at church.

7. Be prepared to stop bad behavior and show a better choice.

Babies, toddlers, and preschoolers don't automatically know which actions are good or bad. Adults must show children the difference. A teacher can say, "Biting hurts! Don't bite. Use words instead. Say, 'Stop!'" (Chapter 6 lists additional discipline ideas.)

8. Praise good behavior and encourage attempts to improve.

Grown-ups are quick to tell children what they have done wrong. Be sure that in God's house children also hear what they have done **right**. Most small children want to please grown-ups. By praising their good behavior, you help preschoolers learn what behavior to repeat in order to please you and God.

Learning to be kind, to take turns, to love one another is a process. For that reason, early childhood teachers also need to watch for and praise both improvement and honest attempts to improve. Say, "Oksana, I can see that you are trying to help Lee build with blocks. God wants us to help each other. You can help by building a tower on this side. Lee, Oksana is being a good church friend to you." This kind of conversation, repeated week after week, helps preschoolers begin to see the benefits of being kind, taking turns, cooperating—being imitators of God.

9. In all activities express your love for the children.

As they grow, the children will find it easier to feel loved by God because Christian teachers like you have shown love for them in God's house—whether their behavior is good or bad.

10. Ask God to help you see the significance of your efforts.

Many adults have a hard time making a connection between changing diapers and nurturing spiritual growth. But Jesus teaches the benefit of menial service. Jesus washed the disciples' feet to teach a spiritual lesson. He also said, "If anyone helps you *by giving you a drink of water* because you belong to the Christ, then he will truly get his reward" (Mark 9:41, *International Children's Bible*, emphasis added).

Can you accept Jesus' opinion of your service? When you serve preschoolers in physical ways, you are taking care of Jesus too (Matthew 18:5,6). What you do faithfully in the nursery and in the preschool class, God will reward openly.

Ministry Check:

Place a checkmark by the routines you already use to nurture love, trust, and obedience in your students. Print an X by routines you want to begin to include when you teach.

1. I look happy to see every child.
2. I arrive before my students and help each child "settle in" to the classroom.
3. I plan a number of brief, interesting activities to teach each lesson.
4. I respond quickly and gently to the physical needs of my students.
5. I plan some time each week to let my students put the Bible lesson into practice.
6. I participate in activities.
7. I stop bad behavior and show a better way.
8. I praise good behavior and all improvements.
9. I express my love for all the children.
10. I ask God to help me see the spiritual significance of my efforts.

Discipline That Is Good 6

Everyone who is fully trained will be like his teacher (Luke 6:40).

Questions To Answer:

1. *What is the purpose of discipline?*

2. *What is preventive discipline?*

3. *What is responsive discipline?*

When I first began teaching, I misunderstood the goal of discipline. I expected a well-disciplined child to sit still, and do whatever the teacher said. I incorrectly thought that children who sat still learned more about God. After all, in public schools children sat in rows of desks while teachers stood and talked.

The preschoolers I taught never lived up to my false ideas about discipline. Even though I liked the children, and they liked me, more than one child cried after I scolded him for wiggling or talking. In those days I was *not* using good discipline.

THE GOAL OF DISCIPLINE

Good discipline is an important part of fulfilling our commission to care for children. In the Great Commission, Jesus told His followers, "Go and make *disciples* of all nations" (Matthew

28:19). The words *disciple* and *discipline* come from the same root word that means "pupil." The goal of Christian discipline is to help children learn to be disciples of Jesus by teaching them what to do as well as what not to do. Christian discipline *influences* pupils to *change their behavior to align with what God says is good.*

Church discipline should differ in some ways from discipline in public schools. The goal of public school discipline is to keep order so education can proceed efficiently. The goal of Christian discipline, on the other hand, is to make disciples. As we make disciples of children, they will follow God's commands as the best pattern for living. For these reasons, Christian discipline centers more on relationship building than public school discipline does. Christian discipline focuses on developing disciples—based on love and trust as well as on obedience.

TWO KINDS OF DISCIPLINE

Good discipline is both **preventive** and **responsive**. The two kinds of discipline are used for different purposes.

Preventive discipline is used before misbehavior. It requires the teacher to organize in such a way that less misbehavior occurs. For example, young children learn from imitation. When preschoolers see others running, biting, or grabbing toys, they are likely to imitate that behavior. By using preventive discipline, a teacher keeps these kinds of activities from starting.

Responsive discipline interrupts and redirects unacceptable behavior. Used correctly, responsive discipline teaches young children what to do as well as what to stop doing. When this kind of responsive discipline is applied long-term, children gradually begin to practice self-discipline.

PREVENTIVE DISCIPLINE IDEAS

As you plan Bible lessons, you can include preventive strategies that will reduce behavior problems in your class. Following are some preventive principles to remember.

Appropriate lesson planning prevents misbehavior. When lesson activities fit children's interests and skills, the need for frequent responsive discipline decreases. Good preparation includes planning for active learning, preparing a comfortable setting, and having enough grown-ups in the room. Chapters 7, 8, 9, and 10 of this handbook give planning ideas like these that will prevent misbehavior.

Communicating the rules prevents misbehavior. All teachers, helpers, children, and parents need to know the rules. It's good to post the rules where adults can be reminded of them. Keep the rules simple and for the good of the children. Here are a few good rules. Use words to settle problems. Share and take turns at church. Don't hurt anyone. Take care of our church. Play with play dough and crayons at the table. Eat at the table.

Good adult examples prevent misbehavior. Jesus' life showed the disciples how to live in God-pleasing ways. Teachers' behavior can play the same role for preschoolers. As you deal with the small children in your class, treat them as you like to be treated. In this way you will introduce the children to living by the "Golden Rule."

Teacher alertness prevents misbehavior. Try to intervene before bad behavior occurs. Misbehavior is often preceded by intensifying body language. Train yourself to be aware of children's body language throughout the room. When teachers are alert to body language of children, they can often avoid misbehavior by redirecting children to better choices. Some young children bite, for example. Once a teacher identifies a child as a biter, the teacher can observe the kind of body language and the kind of tension that usually precedes biting. When a teacher sees those signals, she can step in before anyone is hurt. If Amanda is glaring at a child who took her crayon, the teacher might say, "Amanda, stop! Don't bite! Say, 'That's my crayon.' Chandler, here are crayons for you."

Routines help prevent misbehavior. Grown-ups may find routines boring, but most young children find security in routines. So try out a routine that will fit the learning style of your children. After several weeks modify it if needed. Once you have established a compatible routine for your class, use it consistently. The children will cooperate more quickly because they know what to expect.

Some children need one-on-one attention to prevent misbehavior. Some children don't respond normally. They may have a disability that interferes. Their family life may be in turmoil. They may have inherited a difficult temperament. If most of your students are responding well in class but one child is out of control, that child may need a special worker assigned to him. I remember two very different children who needed this kind of attention.

Jody came to Sunday school in a wheelchair. She had very poor muscle control and couldn't talk. One teacher was assigned to bring learning to Jody in her chair. Jody felt play dough. She saw Bible story visuals. As other children saw Jody receive attention, they grew accepting of this special child. Jody's assigned helper also interacted with other children, but several times during Sunday school, she focused her attention on Jody.

Joshua burst through the door every Sunday. He was full of energy—often destructive energy. Block towers fell. Chairs toppled. Toys broke. None of the normal discipline worked with Joshua. After praying for ideas, we assigned a teacher to work with him. The teacher didn't hover, but she was always aware of Joshua's location and behavior. When Joshua arrived for Sunday school, she greeted him and helped him settle at a learning activity. Then the teacher could help that whole group until Joshua became restless. At that point the teacher would help him find another learning activity. She also sat with Joshua during the Bible story or in worship. Joshua thrived on the relationship he developed with this teacher. Gradually, Joshua learned to control himself.

Positive attention prevents misbehavior. When children don't get attention for good behavior, they will resort to bad attention-getting behavior. As you prepare each lesson, plan ways to give genuine praise. Praise the child who obeys quickly. Praise children who help. Praise the child who is doing better to control himself. Look for genuine ways to praise each child.

GOOD RESPONSIVE DISCIPLINE

Every Sunday school teacher also needs strategies for responsive discipline. Use responsive discipline when a child's behavior is interrupting the lesson, hurting others, endangering himself, or damaging God's house.

The use of responsive discipline requires sensitivity because different children react in different ways to discipline. Discipline that works with a child one week may have no effect at another time. Discipline that improves the behavior of one child may hurt the next child or cause another to act even worse.

Teachers need the Holy Spirit's help to use responsive discipline sensitively. The Holy Spirit knows each child. When the Holy Spirit guides discipline, He gives insights needed to discipline and disciple each little child.

RESPONSIVE DO'S AND DON'TS

The following list of discipline do's and don'ts fit the development of preschool children. Ask the Holy Spirit to direct your use of responsive discipline so children will be influenced to follow God's ways.

Don't expect more than preschoolers can do. Preschool children cannot sit still like grown-ups. They don't know how to share well. They may not have perfect control of bodily functions. They are easily distracted. Don't punish preschoolers for being preschoolers.

Do remind the children of the rules. Preschoolers must be reminded many times of rules before they will begin to remember and obey rules on their own.

Do use the child's name to get his attention.

Do explain briefly to the child what he did wrong. Then describe a better way to behave. Help him start the better behavior, and assure him that God sees him trying to learn good ways to live.

Do redirect behavior whenever possible. If you replace the source of bad behavior with a good activity, the young child will often forget what was causing the problem.

Don't tell children they are bad boys and girls. Instead refer to their *actions* as being wrong. Always remember, God hates sins, but He loves sinners.

Do move to the area of individual misbehavior to correct a child. Your nearness will influence him to obey.

Do discipline in a quiet voice to protect the child's dignity and avoid embarrassing him. A child who is embarrassed in front of his friends may act up more rather than begin to control his behavior.

Don't yell if the group is out of control. When the class is already noisy, your shouts will just add to the clamor. Instead, do something like dimming the lights.

Do say "I'm sorry" if you need to be forgiven by a child for overreacting to bad behavior.

Do consistently enforce the rules. If the rule is "Eat at the table," tell any child who is walking with a snack, "We eat at the table. You can go back to the table to eat, or I'll take your snack to the table for you." The child may choose either option. By enforcing the rules consistently, you'll help the children eventually adopt the rules as their own.

Do catch the children being good. Train yourself to praise good biblical behavior at least as often as you correct bad behavior. Regularly tell the children that God is pleased when He sees them obeying the Bible.

Do stop mistreatment of others. Tell children that you won't allow others to treat them in bad ways either.

Do tell parents about children's good behavior in the children's presence. Help the children come to see themselves as improving all the time.

Don't talk about a child's bad behavior with parents in the child's presence. This kind of talk usually increases, rather than decreases, negative behavior. The child becomes angry or begins to think of himself as a troublemaker (and lives up to the reputation).

Don't ever say, "Jesus doesn't love you when you're bad." That's an unbiblical statement. Romans 5:8 assures us, "God demonstrates his own love for us in this: While we were still sinners, Christ died for us." An important part of loving and trusting God comes from being able to depend on God's and Jesus' love for us—even when we act bad.

THE THINKING CHAIR

If a child persists in misbehavior, go to him and quietly ask him to come with you. Take the student to a child-sized chair that faces classroom activity. Quietly say, "You must sit here and think. Think of good work you would like to do in Sunday school. In a few minutes, I will come back and invite you to join the lesson again." (A playpen serves the same function for a toddler.)

Base the amount of time in the thinking chair on the child's age, using one minute for each year of age. (A 3- year-old would be in the chair for 3 minutes.) At the end of the time-out, return to the child and ask what he has decided to do. During the story time or worship time, your question might be, "Do you want to join us for singing, or do you want to sit in the chair a little longer?" When children are given a choice, they will often choose to cooperate. The teacher decides what choices to offer; when the child chooses, the teacher accepts the choice.

At first some children will not stay seated on the thinking chair. A teacher may need to sit on the chair and hold the child. As the teacher talks softly, most children will settle down. Don't use the chair to embarrass; use the chair to allow time for children to get themselves under control. Children come to understand that if they want the freedom of joining activities they must act responsibly and cooperate with others.

THE IMPACT OF GOOD DISCIPLINE

Every week Carlos spent time in the block center. At 3 years, Carlos could build a better temple than anyone in the class, including the adults. Needless to say, the building efforts of other children frustrated Carlos. He didn't want them to "waste" blocks to build a tower when he could use the same blocks to add another story to his ark. He especially didn't want their towers to topple on his structures. Teachers always reminded Carlos that church is a good place to share with friends, that God wants us to share, and that sharing shows we are growing up inside.

One Sunday while Carlos was building with blocks, two little girls were fighting over a nearby baby swing. Both girls wanted to push a doll in the swing. Neither girl wanted to share. Both girls were yelling. Before the teacher could help, Carlos offered a solution. He asked each girl to back up one step. In that position both girls could push the swing—one pushing it forward, the other backward. After many months of being reminded to share, Carlos began teaching that part of discipline to others.

Use discipline as one of the ways you disciple the little children in your church.

Ministry Check:

Mark the discipline strategies you already use with a checkmark. Mark strategies you want to begin to use with an **X**.

__ I use preventive discipline to reduce misconduct.
__ I use discipline to disciple children.
__ I discipline the children for their benefit.
__ I praise children for good behavior.
__ I tell parents about children's good behavior.
__ I remind children good behavior pleases God.

Plan For Little Children

Jesus said, "Do you truly love me? Take care of my sheep" (John 21:16).

Questions To Answer:

1. *What information do teachers need to know about each child?*
2. *What are good ways to group young children for Christian education?*
3. *What early childhood policies can be used to improve ministry to young children?*

Shortly before Jesus returned to heaven, He gave Peter the task of being a shepherd to Jesus' sheep. Of course, the "sheep" Jesus referred to were believers who needed spiritual guidance just as much as four-legged sheep need physical care. Just as Jesus asked Peter to care for His sheep, teachers are also asked to show their love for Jesus by caring for some of His lambs. Think about your role of teacher-shepherd as you read the following paraphrase of Psalm 23.

The Lord is my *teacher*; He knows all I need.
He helps me draw a green pasture.
He gives me a cup of cool water.
He tells me I've done well.
He teaches me how to live in ways that are good for me.
(Others will see me and want his teaching too.)

Even when I visit a new Sunday school,
I will fear no evil—
For he uses my name to comfort me.
He prepares learning activities for me
I want to do at church.
He notices when I am really trying
And gives me encouragement to keep going.
Surely one lesson will lead to another,
And I will grow in the school of the Lord forever.

In churches of all sizes, preschoolers depend on teacher-shepherds to organize classes for security and learning. The kind and amount of organization generally depends on the size of the "flock." In smaller churches, classes often follow informal guidelines, usually communicated by word of mouth. In larger churches, printed procedures are usually required in order to protect and teach large groups of children. As you read this chapter, select the plans that will benefit the little children that you "shepherd."

BEFRIEND CHILDREN WITH NAME TAGS

Knowing each student's name is an important part of caring for young children. In John 10:3, Jesus says the Good Shepherd calls His sheep by name and they follow Him. We want Sunday school to parallel that kind of individual interest in children. For this reason, it's important that every adult ministering to young children at your church be able to call every child by name.

Name tags come in many shapes and forms. They can be decorative and/or lesson-related, or they can be functional squares of paper. They can be self-adhesive, strung on yarn like pendants, or attached to clothing with loops of tape. For regular members, name tags can be laminated for durability. For babies through 2-year-olds, name tags can be attached to the backs of children so they will leave their identification on.

In addition to using name tags to help children feel at ease, some churches also use name tags to help with recordkeeping. For example, some teachers attach small colored adhesive circles to tags to identify visitors, newly promoted class members, toddlers who are being potty trained, or any other category that teachers need to remain alert to.

ENROLL EACH CHILD

Using enrollment records is one way teachers can come to know their students better. This chapter includes a sample "Preschool Ministry Form."

Some families are sensitive about privacy. Therefore, before asking parents to complete an enrollment form, explain how the information will be used. Emphasize that you want to know each child so you can minister to him at church in a way that matches his needs and interests. If your enrollment form is lengthy, you might ask visiting parents to complete only the first part of the form at church. Then during that week, follow up with a phone call. During your call get to know the parents better and complete the rest of the enrollment form.

PRESCHOOL MINISTRY FORM

Child's First & Last Names _____

Mother's First & Last Names _____

Father's First & Last Names _____

Telephone # _____   Birthday _____

Address _____

Child lives with: ❑both parents ❑mother ❑father ❑guardian

Does child have pet(s)? _____   Pet's name _____

Child's favorite toys or activities: _____

_____

What Bible lesson activities will your child enjoy?

___ hearing stories	___ singing
___ block building	___ shaping play dough
___ drawing/painting	___ cutting/pasting
___ Bible story drama	___ assembling puzzles
___ praying with group	___ movement games

Other Comments: _____

_____

Dates of Follow-Up _____ _____ _____ _____ _____

DECIDE HOW TO GROUP CHILDREN

Young children need to be ministered to in smaller groups than older children. They need more attention in order to feel secure. They need more guidance to get along with others in a group. They need more help to succeed at hands-on activities because they have limited skills.

No matter what size church you attend, the young children need to be taught in relatively small groups. In smaller churches all preschoolers may be grouped together. In larger churches, dividing children into small groups allows them to continue to receive the individual attention they need in order to be happy at church and to thrive spiritually.

CHART NEEDED CLASSES

To decide how to group the preschoolers in your church, gather enrollment records to determine the total number of children from birth through kindergarten who attend your church, including the number of children at each age-level. The class chart in this chapter outlines preschool groupings for churches of various sizes. Adapt these guidelines to match the specific needs of your church and children.

To use the class chart, begin in the left column. Find the box in that column that matches the number of children in your church. Look to the right to see the number of classes needed, what ages to group in each class, whether departments are necessary, etc.

The chart includes some terms that may need to be defined. A class is a group of children in one room with one or more teachers. A department is one or more classes under the leadership of a department coordinator. The coordinator cooperates with teachers to organize supplies, to recruit and train teachers, to organize class schedules, to make room assignments, etc. In a small church, the pastor or Sunday school superintendent may coordinate classes for all age-levels.

CLASS SIZE CHART

For this many children...	*You might organize your Sunday school in this way.*				
	Number of Classes	**Number of Departments**	**Age Groupings**	**Maximum Children Per Class**	**Number of Workers Needed**
1 child (birth thru kindergarten)	1	Combined (birth thru adult)			one teacher to teach one-on-one
1 baby & 1-4 children (ages 2-6)	1	Combined (birth thru adult)	All together (baby through kindergarten)		1 teacher for baby 1 teacher for others
5 to 14 from birth thru kindergarten	2	Start a children's department	**Divide:** babies-2s 3–K	6 10	Begin to team teach: 1 teacher/3 babies 1 teacher/5 students
15 to 29 from birth thru kindergarten	3	Start an early childhood department	**Divide:** babies 1s & 2s 3–K	9 12 20	coordinator 1 teacher/3 babies 1 teacher/ 3 students 1 teacher/4 or 5
30 to 59 from birth thru kindergarten	4	nursery department & early childhood department	**Divide:** babies 1s & 2s 3s & 4s kindergarten	9 12 20 20	dept. coordinators 1 teacher/3 babies 1 teacher/3 students 1 teacher/4 or 5 1 teacher/6 students
60-99 from birth thru kindergarten	5 or more	baby/toddler department preschool kindergarten	**Divide:** babies 1s 2s 3s & 4s kindergarten	9 12 12 20 20	1 coordinator 3 department supervisors 1 for every 3 1 for every 3 1 for every 4 1 for every 5 1 for every 6
100+ from birth thru kindergarten	6 or more	baby dept. 1s dept. 2s dept. 3s dept. 4s dept. kindergarten department (all 5s & some 6s*)	**Divide** babies & toddlers into classes by skills. **Divide** older classes by age with one or more classes at each age.	Form new classes when groups reach maximum sizes shown above.	early childhood minister dept. supervisors Use the same teacher/student ratios as used for smaller churches—all young children need individual attention.

Keep 6-year-olds in kindergarten class until they enter first grade.

TAILOR CLASSES TO CHILDREN'S ABILITIES

The chart suggests grouping some ages in new ways. Work with your pastor, parents, and teachers to determine what groupings will work most effectively in your church. During that process, consider the following groupings.

If space permits, separate crawling babies from younger infants. Once babies begin to crawl, they want to explore, but they have no sense of what is safe for themselves and younger infants. If possible also separate 1-year-olds who are walking well from crawlers. Toddlers with hard-soled shoes can step on the fingers of children who are crawling. At the same time children begin walking, they also begin to understand instructions better and to be more interested in "lessons" in general.

Consider grouping 2-year-olds with 1-year-olds. For the first 6 months after the second birthday, most 2-year-olds are more like 1-year-olds than 3-year- olds. Young 2-year-olds like repetition, with the same lesson being repeated from one week to the next. Many 2- year-olds still put small objects in their mouths and must be protected from small toys that may choke them. Potty training may or may not be in process for young twos.

On the other hand, most 3-year-olds are mature enough to join 4- and 5-year-olds. They're ready for painting projects. Some threes enjoy cutting out simple crafts. They enjoy manipulating small objects that could be hazardous to 2-year-olds. Three-year-olds talk more and can answer more questions. They are capable of jumping, hopping, and climbing at a level similar to 4-year-olds. Overall, 3-year-olds are ready for challenges that would be dangerous or overwhelming for 2-year-olds.

You may be wondering which curriculum to use with these new age groupings. *Baby & Toddler Programs* can be adapted for a combined class of 1- and 2-year-olds by adding an occasional simple art project and by expanding imitation activities a little to fit 2-year-old skills. If 3- and 4-year-olds are grouped, consider using *nursery* materials in that class and reserving *beginner* materials for the kindergarten class.

ESTABLISH MINISTRY POLICIES

Written ministry policies help answer difficult questions. If your early childhood ministry has not developed written policies, consider forming a parent-teacher-pastor committee to complete the task. By answering the following questions in writing, the committee can begin to develop policies to guide early childhood ministries.

1. When will children be promoted to the next class?

For babies and toddlers, many churches promote children by skills—crawling, walking well, potty trained, etc. Older preschoolers are usually promoted in one of three ways: at the end of the spring quarter to coincide with the end of the school year; at the beginning of the fall quarter to parallel opening of school; or at the beginning of the quarter following a child's birthday.

2. Can sick children stay in the church nursery or early childhood classes?

Many churches use a well-child policy. This policy protects children and families from needing to cope with frequent illnesses caught at church.

To create a well-child policy, decide what symptoms constitute a child's being too sick to be with healthy children at church: fever, vomiting, diarrhea, cloudy and green mucous, etc. Return children who have these symptoms to their parents. Always be careful to explain that the policy was developed to keep all the children healthier.

3. How should teachers discipline children?

Discipline strategies found in chapter 6 will help develop this part of a policy. Giving teachers written discipline guidelines insures consistent discipline from service to service. Consistency is one of the most important factors in helping young children to internalize rules that are created for their own good.

4. Who is allowed to check children in and out of early childhood classes?

Small and large churches will probably develop very different policies for this procedure. There are various ways to develop secure check-in/check-out policies. Some churches issue identification cards for parents to show when they pick up their children after church. No child is released unless the person presents the card. Other churches create a check-in and check-out list. Often in these cases, the parent who signs the list when the child arrives is the same parent who must sign the child out after church. Decide what kind of policy is needed in your church in order to assure parents that their children will still be secure when they return for them after each service.

Ministry Check:

Use the list below to begin to decide what policies your early childhood ministries need in order to be "good shepherds" of the children in your church.

Policy	Needed?		In Place?	
Name tags	yes	no	yes	no
Enrollment forms	yes	no	yes	no
Baby care cards	yes	no	yes	no
Class groupings	yes	no	yes	no
Promotion policy	yes	no	yes	no
Health policy	yes	no	yes	no
Discipline policy	yes	no	yes	no
Check-out policy	yes	no	yes	no

Plan For Effective Teachers 8

Do your best to present yourself to God as...a
workman who does not need to be ashamed
(2 Timothy 2:15).

Questions To Answer:

1. What can a church do to recruit enough teachers?

2. What screening procedures are needed to protect preschoolers from potential molesters?

3. What tasks should teachers expect to perform?

4. How can teachers be scheduled to minister to children during church and still grow spiritually themselves?

One of the big challenges to creating an effective Sunday school is finding enough teachers. Here are five ideas that can help to recruit those who will disciple children.

1. Pray for the Holy Spirit's Leading

The Holy Spirit knows each child and each potential teacher. Ask Him to guide the selection of Christians who are, or who can become, effective teacher-shepherds to young children.

2. Create a Vision for Ministry

Help adults in your church understand the long-lasting impact early childhood ministries can make. The first three chapters of this book give this kind of information. Consider creating a mission statement to highlight the focus of early childhood ministry, such as "We Build People—RIGHT from the start!" or "First impressions can last forever!" Share the vision in many ways.

3. Plan To Find Enough Teachers

Young children need individual attention in order to grow spiritually. So keep the following ratios:

For babies........................1 teacher for every 3 babies.
For toddlers & twos........1 teacher for every 3 children.
For preschoolers..............1 teacher for every 5 students.
For kindergartners.........1 teacher for every 6 students.

4. Offer Different Levels of Entry into Ministry

Some adults who hesitate to teach a class may be willing to prepare a room, to prepare lesson materials at home, or to help another teacher. Each level of involvement acquaints potential teachers with ministry to young children and may lead to expanded involvement later.

5. Support Early Childhood Teachers

Help new teachers be successful with young children. Pray for them. Mentor them. Lend them videos to watch. Give them training sheets or books. Take time to call and answer their questions. Pray for them, and find meaningful ways to thank them.

AVOID WOLVES IN SHEPHERD'S CLOTHING

Some volunteers are like wolves in shepherd's clothing. They volunteer to teach not because they want to disciple children but because they plan to sexually abuse them. Since 85% of all sexual abusers are well-known to their victims, churches must be alert to this potential danger without becoming overly alarmed.

Churches have a responsibility before God and the law to protect children at all times and especially within God's house. While churches need policies that protect young children, they also need to avoid overreacting. In order to grow spiritually, children need affectionate relationships with Christian men and women.

Following are the kinds of the guidelines that can protect preschoolers at church. Ask the pastoral staff of your church to establish and supervise policies like these. Check with a lawyer about what policies your community requires.

■ **Every person who cares for babies and toddlers** should complete a confidential worker application. The church should check the references listed on each form.

■ **At least two adults** should work in every enclosed early childhood area. There is safety in numbers.

■ **Diapering stations** in the church nursery should be visible to other workers. No worker should change a diaper in a room alone. Open diapering protects babies and toddlers from possible harm.

■ **Church workers should take** preschoolers to restrooms in groups of at least three—one adult and two children. Safer yet is to assign at two adults at a time to bathroom duty. If only one bathroom fixture is present, one adult can help children wash their hands.

DESIGN MINISTRY DESCRIPTIONS

How will teachers know whether they are successfully discipling preschoolers? One way to assess teaching success is to refer to ministry descriptions. Ministry descriptions help identify duties, set goals for improving skills, and evaluate ministry. This chapter includes a sample early childhood ministry description. Feel free to tailor the description to fit your church.

PROMOTE TEAM TEACHING

In early childhood Christian education, two teachers are usually better than one, even if a class is as small as four students. Team teaching benefits teachers, children, and the church. Team teachers can learn from one another.

E A R L Y   C H I L D H O O D
MINISTRY DESCRIPTION

I accept this teaching ministry in obedience to Jesus' command to make disciples of all people. I commit myself to prayerfully fulfill the goals I have initialed below.

I will come to understand my mission by—

____learning normal age-level traits of my students.

____understanding how young children learn.

____becoming, as much as possible, familiar with each child's interests, abilities, and needs.

I will prepare each lesson by—

____practicing the way I tell each Bible story so children will love God's Word.

____planning each Bible lesson to match the needs and interests of the children in my class.

____choosing hands-on learning activities that help children practice Bible ideas.

I will become a discipler by—

____paying friendly attention to each child.

____being a good example that the children can imitate.

____praising children for genuine effort as well as for achievements.

____evaluating my teaching based on students' responses and on changes in their behavior.

I will be dependable by—

____being present when I am scheduled to teach.

____arriving early so the lesson can begin when the first child comes.

____giving as much advance notice as possible when I must be absent.

Signed: _____

Date: _____

They solve problems together. Team teachers insure that at least one teacher is in the room at all times, even during bathroom times or in emergencies. As discussed earlier, team teachers help safeguard children from abuse. If one teacher must be gone on Sunday, the other teacher can substitute easily. Finally, if one teacher moves or if the class grows and divides, a trained teacher is already in place to make the transition.

DECIDE WHO WORKS WHEN

Every time preschoolers are taught in church, try to insure that most of the children will know at least one of the teachers well. A variety of schedules can be used to insure that at least one teacher will be familiar to the children.

Schedule 1

Some churches teach preschoolers only during the Sunday school hour, keeping the children with parents in all other services. If this is the case at your church, look for a main teacher who will teach Sunday school every week. If more than four children are being taught, remember to find at least one other adult to assist.

Many churches use whole-morning schedules to teach preschoolers. Any of the following staffing schedules can provide consistency for the children while also allowing each teacher to worship in adult services regularly.

Schedule 2

Schedule teams of teachers to minister whole mornings for a month. If three teams are used, each teacher works one month a quarter in preschool classes. This system works better for 4- and 5-year-olds who can remember teachers from earlier months.

Schedule 3

Create a whole-morning team schedule that guarantees at least one worker was in class the previous Sunday. For example, in a class of 15 4- and 5-year-olds, if the team members are:

Worker A—Mai Lin   Worker D—Pat

Worker B—Carmen   Worker E—Deanna

Worker C—Efraim   Worker F—Philippe

Then the workers could be scheduled as follows:

Week 1	Week 2	Week 3	Week 4	Week 5	Week 6	Week 7
ABC	BCD	DEF	EFA	ABC	BCD	DEF

This plan allows every teacher to work two Sundays, then be off for two Sundays. The children still know at least one teacher who was present the previous Sunday.

Schedule 4

Use the same teacher every Sunday during Sunday school; but alternate two teachers, every other Sunday, during worship service. This plan allows all teachers to attend worship at least every other week.

Schedule 5

Consider having one person or one couple per class who work the total morning, from the time Sunday school begins to the end of worship. Other teachers in the room may work only once a month. Some workers may leave after Sunday school or work only during worship service, but the whole-morning person provides security for the children by staying from beginning to end. Schedule total morning teachers to work every other Sunday.

Jesus was a teacher who changed the lives of His students. Then He told His followers to go into all the world and make disciples too. With Jesus' help, your teaching ministry can change the lives of the next generation of the church.

Ministry Check:

Use the "Early Childhood Ministry Description" to evaluate your teaching ministry. Star the tasks you currently do on a regular basis. Highlight any tasks you want to improve in your teaching ministry.

Plan A Room That Welcomes Children

9

> I was glad when they said unto me, Let us go into the house of the Lord (Psalm 122:1, KJV).

Questions To Answer:

1. *How can teachers improve Sunday school rooms despite space and budget limitations?*

2. *Which elements of creating child- friendly Sunday school rooms fit your church setting?*

Children feel welcome at McDonald's. The owners of McDonald's plan their restaurants that way. They know that children can influence parents to come back for Happy Meals again and again. Even before children can talk, some toddlers will begin to clap and point excitedly any time their parents drive by the Golden Arches. The decision-makers at McDonald's have profited by designing facilities with child appeal—facilities that say, "Children are welcome here."

Can the church steeple create the same excitement in preschoolers as the Golden Arches? Yes.

One Sunday morning Lucas' parents grinned broadly as they brought him to Sunday school. Even though this 1-year-old couldn't talk yet, he had communicated to his parents the joy he felt at coming to church. How did he "tell" them without words? When Lucas saw the church from his car seat, he began to clap and laugh and point. Lucas recognized the church building and looked forward to entering his class. Sunday school already held strong appeal to this toddler. He felt welcome there.

DECIDE TO BE RESOURCEFUL

Quite often early childhood teachers feel limited by lack of money. Few, if any, churches are able to spend a McDonald-sized budget on their Sunday school rooms. The "room" Lucas loves, for example, is in one end of a double-wide trailer set next to his church. Parents must walk along a sidewalk in all kinds of weather to deliver children to the facility. Portable dividers, furnishings, and shelves divide the open floor plan into two meeting areas. The carpet needs to be replaced. The only sinks are in the bathrooms.

So what appeals to Lucas about this setting? His teachers have organized the available space to create as much child appeal as possible with the funds available. Lucas is responding to a message sent by the teachers' efforts: "A part of this church is designed so children, just like you, will enjoy learning about God." Rather than be stymied by what they don't have and can't do, Lucas' teachers have emphasized what they can do with available resources.

In any setting, teachers can place their main emphasis on answering this question: "With God's help, what **can** we do to add child appeal to our present facilities." Once you decide to be resourceful, you can look creatively at possibilities for improving the room where you teach Bible lessons.

THE ABCs OF DESIGNING FACILITIES

The English language combines letters of the alphabet to create words that communicate messages. The message "Jesus loves you" combines 13 letters, for example. Making combinations is also a part of creating an appealing classroom. Designing a Sunday school room that children will love involves combining a variety of elements. Every church will not necessarily need all elements, but every Sunday school **can** select **some** elements that will create as much safety and appeal as possible in rooms where children learn about God.

Whether you teach in a garage, on a deck, in a rented hall, or in brand-new facilities, the Holy Spirit can help you improve your "room." As you read through the following "ABCs of Facilities," decide which elements you already use. Then consider which elements you can add or improve to increase the child appeal of the room. Read the ABCs to fill your mind with some possibilities. Then ask the Holy Spirit to guide your thoughts to solutions that will benefit the spiritual growth of the young children in your setting.

A Accessibility

If at all possible, locate early childhood rooms on ground level near sheltered entrances. A convenient location makes it easier for parents to come into the church with babies, toddlers, car seats, diaper bags, blankets, Bibles, and purses. The ground level is also safer for older preschoolers who are not experts at maneuvering stairs.

B Bibles

Purchase several colorful Bibles to keep in class for children to handle and browse. Try to find Bibles that include colorful pictures. Since preschoolers' motor skills are not refined, avoid Bibles with very thin pages. The American Bible Society offers Bibles and Bible portions at reasonable prices.

B Bulletin Boards

Colorful bulletin boards add a great deal of child appeal. Inside the classroom they can reinforce Bible lessons, display children's work, and serve as learning centers. When positioned in halls and foyers, bulletin boards can also inform parents of early childhood topics and promote early childhood ministries to the rest of the congregation. Decorated walls, windows, and even ceilings can function in the same way as mounted bulletin boards. Filling these areas with colorful displays contributes to overall child appeal.

C Color Selection

The use of color can affect learning in subtle ways, so give careful consideration to color selection. In a basement with no windows, for example, light, warm pastel colors like yellow will brighten rooms and make them appear more inviting. On the other hand, colors like blue will visually cool a room that receives too much solar heat through windows. Bright primary colors tend to energize children. To make a room appealing without overstimulating the children, consider using neutral or pastel colors for large areas, such as walls and ceilings, and adding accents with bolder colors.

D Durable

When equipping a preschool room, purchase the most durable items you can afford. Many items that will last when used by only one child, will quickly break in a group setting.

D Diapering Area

If possible, position the diapering area for babies and toddlers near a sink and cover the area with a surface that is easy to clean and disinfect. After each diaper change, it's very important to wash hands with deodorant soap and to disinfect the changing surface, since body wastes can pass many infections. (A solution of 1 part bleach to 10 parts water makes an inexpensive disinfectant.) If no sink is available, use disinfectant wet wipes to clean hands and to wipe the diapering area after each change.

E Equipment

Equipment, such as art easels, baby swings, vinyl mats, play kitchens, and toddler bikes, adds significant child appeal to any room. To become aware of the many options in equipping early childhood rooms, consider requesting a catalog from companies such as: Lakeshore Learning Materials (2695 E. Dominguez St.,

Carson, CA 90749); Environments, Inc. (P.O. Box 1348, Beaufort Industrial Park, Beaufort, SC 29901); or Little Tikes (2180 Barlow Road, Hudson, OH 44236). If even one durable piece of equipment is purchased each year, gradually a room will provide a variety of equipment to use in teaching about Christian living.

E Emergency Plans

Post emergency instructions and evacuation maps in every early childhood room. Create an emergency plan for each kind of emergency common to your locale—tornadoes, earthquakes, floods, fires, and so on. Encourage all teachers and workers to become familiar with the posted plans.

E Electrical Outlets

Curious children can be electrocuted by inserting slender objects into electrical outlets. Simple plastic safety caps can be purchased to cover existing outlets.

F Floor Covering

Carpeting reduces the noise level, cushions falls, and provides a warm surface for the many learning activities children can enjoy while sitting on the floor. However, if you must choose between spending money for carpeting or equipment, seriously consider using a less expensive floor covering in order to purchase more equipment. If the church budget can afford both carpeting and equipment, cover two-thirds of the room with carpet and one-third with vinyl. Place the vinyl in areas where children will be painting, using play dough, etc.

F Furnishings

If a room is wall-to-wall furnishings, the kinds of active learning will be restricted. By removing a large table from a small room, teachers can promote more versatile use of available space. Some churches purchase or build lap trays that can be stacked when not in use. Rather than using chairs in a small room, children can sit on the floor or on carpet squares to hear Bible stories.

F Flannelboard

If you decide to allow children to sit on the floor for story times, consider two alternatives to tall easel-mounted flannelboards. **Option 1:** Hem a 4- by 3-foot rectangle of flannel or sweatshirt material. Use construction staples or finishing nails to permanently attach the rectangle (fuzzy side out) to a wall near the group activity area. **Option 2:** Cut triple thicknesses of corrugated cardboard into 3- by 5- foot rectangles. Fold the rectangles into 3- by 2 1/2-foot "tents" that stand on their own. Cover both sides of each tent with velour or one of the previously suggested fabrics. Prepare for the story by setting the flannelboard tent on the floor and arranging needed visuals on the backside of the tent. As the story is told, visuals can be transferred to the front.

G Germ-Free Setting

In group settings, like Sunday school and church, children can be exposed to a variety of contagious diseases. By following good sanitation procedures, teachers reduce the probability of children's passing diseases to one another. In addition to the cleaning suggested under "Diaper-Changing Areas," teachers can set aside any toy that has been mouthed by a child. Before returning the toy for general use, it should be washed with warm soapy water and air dried. Permanently remove any toys that cannot be laundered or washed. Clean all floors thoroughly on a regular basis.

Germs are passed along more by dirty hands than any other means, so encourage handwashing among children and teachers. Washing hands with deodorant bar soap will effectively kill germs. Teachers should wash their hands before beginning to work with children and before serving snacks. They should also wash their hands after wiping a runny nose, helping a child with toileting, cleaning vomit, or treating a bleeding wound.

G Group Activity Circle

In almost every Sunday school, children will gather for singing, worship, the Bible story, or some other group activity. Since preschoolers usually lack a sense of order, teachers can plan the room in a way to give order to group activities. Colorful plastic tape, for example, can be used on the floor to form a large circle. At group time the teacher(s) can invite children to sit around the edge of the circle. The circle allows all children to see without looking around anyone. If children wiggle off the line, teachers can remind children to sit on the line. The circle can also make it easier for children to stand in a circle to play games.

H Heating & Cooling

When preschoolers feel too warm, they tend to become restless and irritable. When they feel too cool, preschoolers may be more aware of shivering than of learning. If your Sunday school room is too warm or too cool, ask church leaders to problem solve with you. Can weather stripping or curtains be added to windows? Can cracks be caulked? Does a church member have the ability to install a ceiling fan? While you may not be able to completely control room temperature, you can improve it with some relatively low-cost maintenance.

I Instruments

Rhythm instruments help children worship. Maracas, tambourines, xylophones, small keyboards, and even rhythm instruments for babies can all be purchased in stores or catalogs. Toys can also be used as instruments. Children can tap two blocks while singing. They can pat tabletops or shake rattles. Some rhythm instruments can be made. Nearly empty salt cartons can be covered with contact paper for shakers, or dry cereal can be sealed in film canisters. Large jingle bells can be firmly sewn to elastic wristbands. Any of these variations can help children make joyful sounds to the Lord.

J Jesus

Look for a variety of ways to display pictures and visuals of Jesus in the room. Ask other teachers to save outdated posters and visuals of Jesus for undated use in preschool rooms. Attach laminated pictures of Jesus to walls at the children's eye level. Create simple games to use with the pictures. Provide colorful picture books about Jesus' life.

K Kid's Kitchen

In a child-sized play kitchen teachers can help the children act out godly responses to common family events. If finances prevent purchasing play kitchens, teachers can decorate cardboard boxes to look like kitchen appliances. In a small room, dollhouse furnishings or Little Tike figures can be used on the table to act out family scenes.

K Kit For First Aid

Highly active and slightly uncoordinated preschoolers tend to be accident-prone. To treat minor injuries, purchase or assemble a first aid kit for each room. Include such items as Band-Aids, antiseptic ointment, an ice bag, gauze for cleaning cuts, and surgical gloves to wear when treating bleeding wounds. Any items that touch blood should be disposed of in sealed, double plastic bags.

L Lighting

Lighting affects children's emotional responses to a room. In the church nursery, dim lighting or adjustable lighting can help babies and toddlers rest more peacefully. Bright lighting is better in older preschoolers' rooms, however, since a dim room may seem dingy or uninviting. If your room seems too dark, the solution may be as simple as a higher watt bulb. If the room needs even more light, inquire about the new kinds of fluorescent or halogen light fixtures or about adding more fixtures, such as wall lamps.

M Multi-Function Rooms

In many churches, rooms are used for several purposes. If you teach in a room that is shared by other ministries, try to establish communication with the other groups. Using appropriate channels, negotiate who will use which bulletin boards, which equipment, which supplies, which storage areas, and so on. Clear communication can lead to cooperation between ministries who meet in one room. Clearly labeled storage units, for example, can insure that shared supplies are always stored in the same place and are available for all ministries when needed.

M Mirror

Wall-mounted mirrors make it easier for preschoolers to learn by imitation. Children can imitate one another's movements and expressions in a mirror. They can see how they look when dressed up like Bible characters. The reflective quality of a mirror can also brighten a dim room or make a small room seem larger. Even so, mirrors raise safety concerns when used in early childhood facilities. No glass mirrors should be installed. Instead look for mirrored Plexiglas that can be purchased by the foot from plastics retailers. Check in the Yellow Pages under "plastics." Since Plexiglas scratches easily, it must be cleaned only with warm water and soft cloths, not with window cleaners or paper towels.

N Nature Center

When properly supervised, a nature center allows children to use their God-given senses to explore parts of God's creation. Consider keeping an aquarium or terrarium in the center at all times. Depending on your locale, the nature center for 3-year-olds and up can rotate such objects as colored leaves, pinecones, shells, fruit, seeds, rocks, and so on. Decide whether the items will be available at all times or only when a teacher is nearby to supervise.

O Outdoor Equipment

If a safe area is available, preschoolers can learn a lot about God by spending some time outdoors during nice weather. Children can create Bible landscapes in sand. They can help one another walk along balance beams. They can pretend to travel from Egypt to Canaan. The kinds of equipment used for outdoor activities can range from temporary cardboard boxes, to hand-made sand boxes and tire swings, to molded plastic indoor-outdoor sets, to expensive commercial equipment. Unanchored swingsets are not safe in group settings. The companies listed under "equipment" in this chapter sell sturdy outdoor equipment.

O Odors

Children and adults react strongly to odors. Some aromas, like popcorn, mint, or perfume make a room seem more inviting. Other odors, like mildew, soiled diapers, or aging food make us want to leave a room. Stay alert to any dominant odors in a classroom. If a distasteful odor exists, decide how to eliminate it. Diapers can be placed in double plastic bags. Mildew can be removed with a bleach solution. Food can be stored in airtight containers. To create inviting smells, add mint extract to homemade play dough or wear a subtle pleasant fragrance.

P Pegs

Wall-mounted pegs provide handy storage in rooms. In nurseries, diaper bags can hang on pegs. In preschool rooms paint smocks, dress-up clothes, or children's coats can hang on pegs. Fresh smocks for teachers can also hang on pegs. (Launder smocks after every use.) Try to mount some pegs at the children's level so they can hang up their belongings.

Q Quiet Area/Retreat

Some preschoolers need an area where they can retreat from the high activity level of a group. This is especially true when groups stay in one room for over an hour. A "quiet retreat" can be created many ways. A blanket thrown over a table can create a temporary tent for reading or relaxing. A large cardboard box can create a small room within a large room. Two low bookcases placed perpendicularly from corner walls can separate a little book corner from the main area of the room while still being visible to teachers. Even a teacher in a rocking chair can provide a soothing setting for a child who wants to relax and look at Bible pictures or sing quiet worship songs. Examine your room for an area where children can enjoy some quiet time while at church.

R Restrooms

It's ideal if restrooms with child-sized fixtures adjoin preschool rooms. This location allows teachers to more easily manage frequent toileting required by preschoolers. It also allows better accountability of adults as they work with children in restroom settings. If restrooms don't adjoin the preschool area, try to use classrooms that are near adult restrooms. Easily removed and stored seat adaptors can be snapped on adult-sized fixtures to allow small children to feel more secure.

S Storage

For teaching supplies, off-the-floor storage works best in early childhood rooms. Wall-hung cabinets keep teaching supplies out of the children's reach without taking up valuable floor space. On the other hand, toys should be stored on low, open shelves where children can reach them. Avoid using toy boxes for storing toys. Toys are hard to find when buried in a toy box, and children can be hurt if hinged lids fall on fingers or heads.

S Space

Young children learn on the go. They need room to move in a variety of ways. When room assignments are being considered, encourage church leaders to *assign rooms by activity level rather than by the size of the students*. Active preschoolers actually need more room than older church members. One church manual recommends the following:

Babies & Toddlers .... 35 square feet per pupil
Preschoolers .... 30 square feet per pupil
Elementary .... 25 square feet per pupil
Youth .... 20 square feet per pupil
Adults .... 15 square feet per pupil

T Traffic Patterns

Especially in large rooms try to carefully design traffic patterns. For example, what will children see when they first come into the room? If items with high appeal are positioned near the door, children may more easily separate from parents and come into Sunday school. Will late arrivals distract children in group activities? Try to position the group activity area away from the door in order to reduce visual distractions during story and worship times. Where will children store personal items? If possible, position personal possessions near the door for easy access when children arrive and leave. Will building blocks be knocked over by passing children? Locate the block area in a corner where the children's work will be protected from accidental topples and where blocks are less likely to be scattered throughout the room. Examine your room for similar concerns.

U Uncluttered

Most young children are unorganized; so when they work with toys, they create clutter. Teachers can help control clutter by planning ways for children to be more organized. Consider using plastic tape to divide tabletops. The lines will help children stay within their own space when using table activities. Also bring individual containers to hold sets of toys like pegs, stringing beads, interlocking blocks, puzzles, etc. Storage carts on wheels or sturdy cardboard boxes can be used to collect wood blocks. Even crayons and scissors will stay more organized in little bins. Make a practice of encouraging children to help return toys and supplies to their containers after using them.

V Ventilation

A stuffy room tends to make children drowsy. Ceiling fans can be used to move air. Freestanding fans should be avoided, since young children may run into them or can catch fingers or small toys in fan blades. If windows provide ventilation, be sure children cannot fall out.

W Water

Preschool children need to drink water more frequently than adults. If no water fountain is available, serve water from a covered, plastic pitcher in small paper cups for every session. In addition, water is needed to wash hands and clean up after art activities. If no sink is available, use a shallow plastic tub containing an inch or two of water for cleanups.

X X-Out Broken Equipment

Young children are not alert to potential hazards of broken toys and equipment, so teachers need to be.

Continually stay alert for broken toys that could hurt young children. If the toys cannot be repaired, dispose of them. Also inform church leaders or maintenance personnel when equipment or furnishings need repairs.

Y Yes-Orientation

Evaluate the preschool Sunday school room from a child's point of view. Is it OK for a child to touch and handle whatever is at his level? Or are a number of items "out of bounds" even though they are within reach? As much as possible try to make "no-no's" inaccessible to children. Let the items within children's reach be inviting and enjoyable to use as you teach the children about God and Jesus.

Z Zoning

Young children love to run in large open spaces, but running in group settings usually leads to bumps and bruises. Rather than line the walls with furnishings, bring them out into the center of the room to create zones for different kinds of activities. The zones will help focus children's attention on activities and will save teachers from giving constant reminders to slow down.

Z Zeal

The teacher's zeal to make church attractive to young children is the most important element of creating Sunday school rooms with child appeal. With inspiration from the Holy Spirit along with determination and resourcefulness, a teacher with zeal can transform *any* room into a part of the church that says, "Jesus loves children, and children are welcome here!"

The "Facilities ABC List" is not comprehensive. If your church is ready to expand on the basics of a room, consider ordering school supply catalogs to use as references for ideas. The materials offered by school supply companies are usually durable enough to be long-lasting, even with a group of active preschoolers.

Ministry Check:

Read through the "Facilities ABCs" and check off the components already being used effectively in your classroom. Write an "X" by elements you can work on to enhance the room for children. Consider ranking the latter elements by priority. Then approach the leadership of your church to propose your suggestions for adding more safety or child appeal to part of God's house.

Plan Lessons That Fit Your Students 10

I try to please everybody in every way...so that they may be saved (1 Corinthians 10:33).

Questions To Answer:

1. *How does "thinking like a child" help teachers plan more effective Bible lessons?*

2. *What five parts of early childhood Bible lessons are described in this chapter?*

3. *Why should teachers plan hands-on learning for each lesson?*

In 1 Corinthians 10:23–33, Paul writes about how Christians influence one another. According to Paul our influence on one another can be positive or negative. Paul ends by saying that he plans to live to please everyone—even when that means modifying his own behavior. Paul chose to adapt to the needs of others so that as many people as possible could be saved under his influence.

Sunday school lessons that are planned to fit the way young children learn will influence them to live for God. Poorly planned Sunday school lessons influence children too. Children may be influenced to think the Bible is too hard to understand. They may be influenced to believe that the Bible is only for Sunday. They may be influenced to conclude that Sunday school is boring. How a teacher approaches lesson planning makes a big difference in how Bible lessons will influence children.

THE SUNDAY SCHOOL SCHEDULE

No matter what church a preschooler attends, certain elements will probably be found in each Bible lesson. The time spent in each part of the lesson will depend on (1) the children's interests and (2) the length of the total session. The columns below list the common elements of early childhood Bible lessons. A time range is suggested for each lesson segment. These suggested times will work in sessions that last from 45 to 90 minutes:

LESSON SEGMENT	TIME
Opening Activities	10 to 20 minutes
Worship Activities	5 to 15 minutes
Bible Story Activities	10 to 20 minutes
Practice Activities	15 to 25 minutes
Closing Activities	5 to 10 minutes

The rest of this chapter will suggest ways to plan each lesson segment. The first section of opening activities is covered with the most detail. Many of the same principles used to plan opening activities can be transferred to make decisions about worship, the Bible story, practice activities, and closing.

OPENING ACTIVITIES

During lesson preparation every teacher needs to decide how to help children "leave behind" the events leading up to church and begin looking forward to the Bible lesson of the day. Every class will need this kind of refocusing activity, but the specifics will vary from church to church.

In some churches, teachers may need to serve a nutritious snack to hungry children as soon as they arrive. Public educators have learned that hungry children cannot concentrate on learning, so many public schools begin by serving breakfast before teaching lessons. If the children in your class are likely to come to church hungry, then your first form of ministry may be the physical one of offering a glass of water and a nutritious snack in Jesus' name (Mark 9:41).

In most classes, however, children will have eaten before church. In these churches teachers will need to plan one or more high-interest, hands-on opening activities that will focus children's attention on the Bible lesson. When choosing such activities, consider the following: (1) the likes and dislikes of your particular children; (2) whether children are likely to arrive at the same time or to come a few at a time over a 10- to 15-minute period; and (3) the number of teachers and amount of space available. Let's go through these considerations one by one.

What do your students like and dislike?

Do the students in your present class seem energetic and ready to play when they first arrive? Then plan one or more opening activities that will allow them to enjoy moving during the first minutes of class while introducing them to the Bible lesson. If, for example, the Bible story is about Mary and Joseph traveling to Egypt, you might use masking tape to make "roads" on a tabletop. Show children how to move toy cars along the tape roads, making different sound effects. Then begin talking about trips the children have taken with their families, about how we travel today compared to the way families traveled in Jesus' day, and about different reasons families take trips. This kind of **guided conversation** helps children begin to think about the trip that will be described in the Bible story.

Many other "play," or "action-oriented" options could be used to open a lesson about the trip to Egypt. The children could move around a tape circle as if flying in planes, swaying on camels, jouncing on donkeys, bouncing in buses, etc. After each action the children could decide if that was a possible way Mary and Joseph could have traveled. At another church, children could build pyramids in one corner of the room with blocks, or they could pack in the homeliving center to prepare for a trip. **In each case, the teacher would use guided conversation about the activity to begin to focus the children's attention on**

some aspect of the week's Bible lesson.

If your children arrive sleepy or grumpy, on the other hand, you may need to plan quiet opening activities that will ease the children into the lesson. Instead of using big muscles to build with blocks or to move in a circle, drowsy children may prefer to glue paper pyramids, palm trees, and stars to a large paper background to use later as a backdrop for Bible story visuals. They might want to use play dough to shape pretend food that Mary and Joseph might eat on a trip. The teacher would still guide conversation during the quiet activities. Because whether the opening activity is active or quiet, the goal is to begin to focus the children's attention on the Bible story and lesson.

Will the children arrive together at the same time or individually during an extended period of time?

If children in your class arrive at various times, plan opening activities that can begin with the first child but also can be joined by latecomers. Several of the activities mentioned earlier fit this category. The tabletop roads, building-block pyramids, Bible story background, and play dough foods can all be joined in process.

By beginning as soon as the first child arrives, you immediately take control of what is happening in your class. Remember, if the teacher does not have something planned for the first child, he will find something to do; and it probably will not be related to the Bible story. Once early arrivals are interested in *unguided* play activities, it will be more difficult to persuade them to cooperate with the teacher's lesson plans. So put your opening plans into effect when the first child comes.

As other children arrive later, invite them to come and join the activity. Encourage the children who are already working to help show the new arrivals what to do. This strategy begins to use children as "ministers" to one another. The children who come later will feel welcomed by their friends. The children who come earlier will feel like important helpers to the teacher.

How much space and how many teachers are available?

If you teach alone in a small room, then opening time will probably be one activity that can be done **on a table or while standing** in a small area of the room. Of the opening options mentioned earlier, the tape roads, play dough food, and Bible story background could all be done in this setting. Most of the other options could also be used in this setting—with modifications. One suitcase could be packed on the table, for example; or children could sit in chairs and pretend to bounce along in a bus or on a camel.

In a larger room with a team of teachers, opening may become a choosing time of several activities. Station one teacher near the door to welcome each child, to list the opening options, and to help each child decide which activity to join. Each remaining teacher would be in charge of one opening activity. So in this setting, some children would be building block pyramids while others make play dough food and still others pack in the homeliving area. The teacher in charge of each activity guides the conversation, as described earlier, to focus the children's thinking on some part of the Bible lesson. The children are allowed to move from one opening activity to the next until it's time for the worship lesson segment.

A Word About Giving

As preschoolers bring offerings to Sunday school, help them give the money as soon as they arrive. If their money isn't given right away, children may lose it and be sad later. In the youngest classes there is also danger that coins could be swallowed.

When planning for giving, it's important to once again think about the process not only from a biblical point of view but also as a child is likely to think. The Bible says that God loves a cheerful giver. Try to think of an interesting giving activity to go with each Bible story. In the lesson about going to Egypt, for example, children might place their money in the back of a toy pickup and "drive" it down one of the tape roads to a church bank to deposit. For young children, it's more important that they feel happy about giving to God than that they follow the adult style of dropping money into the same offering container each week.

Making Transitions

Teachers can use several strategies to help make transitions easier for children to make.

First, give the children a 3-to 5-minute "warning" that another activity will start soon. You might flick the lights and say, "Soon we will stop our work and come to worship." This signal gives the children time to finish what they are doing and begin thinking about what will come next.

Second, either create a permanent routine for changing activities, or plan new lesson-related fun ways to move from one lesson segment to another.

If you choose to develop a permanent transition routine, you will use the same method each time one lesson segment ends and another begins—week after week. The routine might be a song that tells children what to do next. It could be a recorded tune. It might be turning lights on and off. Or it could involve giving a sticker or stamp to each child as he arrives for the next activity.

Whatever the routine, try to choose one that children will enjoy for a long time.

You could decide to plan a variety of transitions related to each lesson. If so, you will reinforce the lesson each time you move from one lesson segment to the next. In the lesson about Jesus' traveling to Egypt, for example, you might use a Follow-the-Leader game to gather the children. You could move around the room singing the following words to the tune of "The Bear Went Over the Mountain":

> Come join the trip I am taking.
> Come join the trip I am taking.
> I want my friends to go with me—
> Come take this trip with me.

This song would be too simple and repetitious for any other age, but preschoolers will enjoy it since it's connected to a game. Preschoolers love games. As the children come to expect that cooperating with the teacher will be fun, they will be prepared to do what you say more quickly.

WORSHIP ACTIVITIES

When planning the worship segment of each lesson, it's once again important for teachers to think like little children. Why? Worship will be more genuine for little ones if they are allowed to worship in childlike ways. When Jesus rode into Jerusalem, children waved palm leaves to worship Him. When mothers brought their children for Jesus to bless, He took them up into His arms. Jesus even said that we all need to become like little children in order to enter the kingdom of God. So when children sing action songs or repeat rhyming prayers, God accepts these childlike actions as genuine worship.

Songs of Worship

Preschool children usually like to sing, especially if the songs include enjoyable actions, an appealing melody, and repetitious words. Simple songs that repeat a few meaningful phrases are easier for younger preschoolers to learn. By the time children are 4 or 5 years old, though, they also enjoy the challenge of learning a *few* songs with trickier words. Both older and younger preschoolers enjoy listening and doing actions to some complex but interesting songs without necessarily trying to sing along.

Preschoolers like action songs because they are fun to do. But actions also help nonreading preschoolers understand and learn the words more quickly. Don't be surprised if younger preschoolers either sing or do the actions. At first, preschoolers can do only one thing at a time. Action songs tend to energize preschool children. For that reason, it's generally good to **begin** singing time with these fast-paced songs. **End** with slower paced songs that will prepare the children to sit quietly to say a prayer or hear a story.

Especially, if you teach toddlers or 2- or 3-year- olds, consider interspersing songs throughout your teaching rather than singing all songs at one formal time. Children are more likely to follow musical instructions. If you want the children to stack blocks to make a "church," for example, you might sing the following words to the tune of "Bringing in the Sheaves."

> Building up the church.
> Building up the church.
> We will come rejoicing.
> Building up the church.

The melody and the rhythm of a song will help draw younger children's attention more quickly to what you are teaching. Second, the tunes will help children want to repeat learning activities. Music is one way to transfer learning from the Sunday school room to the living room.

Prayers

Use prayer times in lessons both to pray and to teach about prayer. Each time you lead the children in prayer, share *one* idea about prayer like the following. Prayer is talking with God. God wants us to talk to Him. God enjoys hearing us talk to Him every day. We can talk to God anywhere. Sometimes we don't even need to talk out loud; God can read our prayer thoughts. Sometimes when we talk to God, we can thank Him for good things we like in our homes, in our church, or in the world. Sometimes we can tell God what we like about Him or Jesus. Sometimes we can ask God to help us or someone we know.

Remember you are trying to teach children to pray throughout the week as well as at church. By teaching children a number of ways and times to pray, you will help establish a rich prayer life for children. A song can be a prayer. One sentence can be a prayer. A prayer can be repeated after a teacher. Sometimes a prayer may rhyme. In addition to praying at specific prayer times, like before eating snacks or after the Bible story, it's also good to watch for spontaneous prayer moments—while a child pets a kitten created by God, when a child cries over a scraped knee, when a child paints a colorful picture about a Bible story.

THE BIBLE STORY & RELATED ACTIVITIES

Just as the sermon is the core of the adult worship service, the Bible story is the heart of each Bible lesson in early childhood Sunday school. Adult sermons may last from 15 to 60 minutes.

A Bible story for young children must be much shorter, however, in order to fit the way children think, talk, and act. Just as preschoolers like brief, colorful picture books rather than thick, heavy textbooks, preschoolers also need to hear short, active Bible stories, not lengthy "sermons."

A commonly accepted rule of thumb for children's attention span *during listening activities* is:

> *One minute of attention for each year of age!*

A 1-year-old will probably pay attention to a story for 1 minute; a 5-year-old, for 5. Most teachers want to spend more than 1 to 5 minutes per lesson in Bible teaching; yet, most preschoolers cannot listen for more than 1 to 5 minutes. What's a teacher to do?

Once again, an early childhood teacher will benefit from thinking as a child is likely to think. When it comes to keeping children's attention, Christian teachers can learn from *Sesame Street*. At the end of each TV program, one of the characters says, "This program was brought to you by the letter *M* and the number *3*." Throughout that program the letter *M* and the number *3* were taught over and over again in *different, interesting, brief* ways. At church, Bible stories also need to be taught to preschoolers in many *different, interesting, brief* ways.

Chapter 11 of this handbook suggests Bible story methods that will help get and keep young children's attention for Bible stories.

PRACTICE & APPLICATION ACTIVITIES

Preschoolers need practice. Babies need practice to learn to walk. Toddlers need practice to learn to talk. Preschoolers need practice to learn to pedal a trike or a bike. Yet when it comes to spiritual lessons many churches tell Bible stories and show Bible visuals and expect children to sink or swim spiritually without any **practice** in Christian living.

This is a very serious shortcoming. Recent studies have shown that when it comes to making moral choices children who grow up in a church are almost as likely to cheat or lie, for example, as children with no church training. I believe that part of this sad sameness comes from two principles. (1) *Knowing* what is right does not necessarily equal *doing* what is right. (2) Church lessons are often so different from everyday living that *children don't transfer what they learn on Sunday to how they live during the week.*

Teachers who want their students to live out Bible lessons need to prayerfully plan application and practice activities for each lesson. Chapter 12 of this handbook describes how to use practice activities to help preschoolers in your class begin to live in godly ways even before they learn to read or write.

Snacks & Memorization

Whenever possible, plan a snack that fits the Bible story. In the lesson about going to Egypt, children could make and eat trail mix. Use guided conversation to connect the snack with the Bible story in the children's thinking. Snacks can also be used effectively while telling the Bible story. As you prepare each story, ask yourself, "What food could I use during this story?" You might give each child a paper towel to use as a fishnet; then, when Jesus' friends catch fish, lay fish crackers on the "net." Animal crackers can go with the stories of the ark, creation, and the first Christmas. Pretzels can be barley Ruth collected or frosted flakes can be manna. Even cotton candy can be used during the story of God's leading His people with a cloud.

Use play activities to teach Bible verses. In the lesson about going to Egypt, the children might walk on a tape circle, saying a word of the verse with each step. Or they could repeat the verse before coming down a slide. For kindergarten children a teacher could print the Bible verse on two posterboard pyramids. She could cut one pyramid into puzzle pieces for kindergartners to assemble by matching shapes to the complete pyramid. The teacher would point to each word and help the children repeat the verse on the completed puzzle. There are many fun ways to teach a Bible verse. Interesting activities help children look forward to learning God's Word.

CLOSING ACTIVITY

For many preschoolers, their parents' location during church is a mystery. Some preschoolers wonder whether their parents will return as promised. As soon as the first parent arrives after church, most young children will start mentally preparing to leave. If a child's homelife has been affected by change, such as a recent move, the arrival of a new baby, or family turmoil of any kind, he may feel anxious about being "abandoned." From an adult perspective this fear may seem groundless, but from a preschooler's point of view being left may seem a real possibility.

A teacher who can think like a child about closing time will plan to reduce these anxieties. One effective way to help children remain happy to the end of church is to plan an enjoyable closing activity for each lesson.

In several ways, the closing activity is just the reverse of the opening activity. For instance, children may leave a few at a time rather than as a group. If that is true, you will want to plan an activity that can continue even as children are leaving. In the story about traveling to Egypt, one such activity might be a Bible story review using visuals. Let a child arrange all the story visuals on the flannel board. Then ask the others to close their eyes while one visual is removed. After opening their eyes, they should try to guess the missing visual. Use guided conversation to remind the children of the significance of the visual they guessed. Repeat the process until all children have left.

Bible lessons that truly help preschoolers grow spiritually will be very different from lessons for any other age. When teachers plan lessons that fit each student's needs and development, they help each child learn how to live to please God from the beginning of life. They train a child in the way he should go.

Ministry Check:

To help you plan lessons that fit the children in your class, complete the following profile. Check all that apply.

OPENING:

1. When my students arrive, they are: ___ hungry; ___ sleepy; ___ frightened; ___ ready to go.
2. With the current teacher(s) and space, I/we could plan the following number of opening activities at a time: ___ 1; ___ 2; ___ 3; ___ 4; ___ other.

WORSHIP:

1. I believe my students would enjoy singing at the following time(s): ___ worship time; ___ story time; ___ activity time; ___ closing time.
2. I could pray with children at the following times: ___ opening; ___ worship; ___ before snack; ___ when they're hurt; ___ at moments of wonder.

STORY:

1. My students would enjoy being involved in the Bible story in the following ways: ___ using puppets; ___ holding Bibles; ___ pretending to move like characters; ___ making sound effects; ___ answering questions; ___ repeating words and sounds; ___ acting out the story.

PRACTICE:

1. Based on room size and number of teachers, I/we can plan the following kinds of practice: ___ tabletop activities; ___ homeliving; ___ Bible dress-up; ___ blocks; ___ creation center; ___ books; ___ snack; ___ Bible memorization; ___ movement ; ___ art.

CLOSING:

1. At closing time my students: ___ leave all at once; ___ leave a few at a time; ___ seem calm; ___ seem anxious.

Telling Techniques— Storytelling

11

We will tell the next generation the praise-worthy deeds of the Lord. (Psalm 78:4)

Questions To Answer:

1. *How do Bible stories develop faith in children?*

2. *What techniques can teachers use to keep preschoolers' attention during Bible stories?*

In Psalm 78 God commands His people to tell Bible stories to their children. Psalm 78 lists some stories children should hear about God: how He divided the Red Sea; how He led His people with a cloud and fire; how God made water flow from a rock; how He sent manna to eat. God says that if children learn these stories, they will come to trust God and want to obey Him (Psalm 78:7). Storytelling, therefore, is part of God's strategy for passing faith from generation to generation. Every time an early childhood Sunday school teacher tells a Bible story, she follows God's plan for passing faith to a new generation—for helping children love, trust, and obey God.

Successfully telling a Bible story to preschoolers calls for different skills from preaching a sermon to adults or telling a story to elementary children. Preschoolers don't sit still long. They want to touch the visuals. They complain if they can't see. They jostle one another. They interrupt with unrelated questions. One or two wander off during the story, and someone always needs to "go" right after the story starts.

While these interruptions make telling Bible stories more challenging for teachers, they represent normal behavior for preschool children. Since we want preschoolers to love Bible stories, we must find and use storytelling techniques that match the way young children normally listen. We want to hear little children say, "Tell that story again!"

PRESCHOOL STORY GROUPINGS

As much as possible, teachers should arrange seating at story time so everyone can see without being crowded. In small and medium groups, sitting with the children in a circle will allow everyone a clear view of the visuals. If children are sitting on the floor, colorful plastic tape can be used to create a story circle. At story time everyone can be invited to sit on the circle. If a child moves too close to the visuals and blocks the view of others, he can be reminded to return to the circle. In large classes, teachers can tell and retell the Bible story to a few children at a time. This small-group approach benefits children in several ways. Preschool children need individual attention. In a large class, it's too easy for a preschooler to become lost in the crowd. By telling the Bible story to small groups of children, teachers can give individual attention combined with God's truth from the Bible. When children hear stories in small groups, they have more opportunity to ask questions, touch visuals, and participate in the story than they would in a large group. The small group reduces sensory distractions, since fewer children are involved, and increases children's ability to focus on the story.

STORYTELLING TIPS

Teachers often overestimate how long students can concentrate on listening. A variety of storytelling techniques or tips can extend the time children stay interested in each Bible story. By using these techniques teachers can devote more time in each Sunday school session to teaching, not just telling, the Bible story without placing unrealistic expectations on the children.

Tip #1: Involve the children actively in each story.

Since preschoolers need to move often, direct their movements toward the Bible story. When planning the Bible story, think of related actions children can do, sounds they can make, or props they can move that will help to tell the story. For example, in the story of the Children of Israel in the wilderness, even toddlers can move toy people on a tabletop as if they're walking to a new home. In the story of Jesus' stilling the storm, older preschoolers could shake sheets of paper, gently at first to sound like sails in a breeze, then fast and hard to sound like sails flapping in a storm. These kinds of involvement not only help keep children's attention, but also help young listeners imagine themselves actually "living" the events of the story. The Bible stories seem more real to children.

Tip #2: Appeal to the children's five senses.

When God created us, He gave us five ways to learn: hearing, seeing, touching, tasting, and smelling. The more Bible stories are taught in ways that involve children's senses, the more the children will remember, believe, and obey the Bible. If children only hear a story, they will probably remember only 10%. If children hear and see a Bible story, they are likely to remember 50%. But if the children hear, see, and do a Bible story, they will probably remember 90%.

During preparation to tell Bible stories teachers should plan ways to appeal to different senses. A teacher who is preparing to tell toddlers the story of the Children of Israel in the wilderness, for example, may want to buy oyster crackers to lay on a tabletop to represent the manna God sent for His people to eat each day. During the story, toddlers will be able to collect and taste food just as people in the Bible did. By including tasting of food in the story, the teacher increases the likelihood that her young listeners will remember the story and want to hear it again.

There are many, many ways to involve children's senses in Bible stories. Children can add sound effects to stories by patting their legs, or repeating a designated sound every time a certain word is used in the story. Methods that appeal to sight include coloring large backgrounds for visuals or dressing up to look like characters in the story. Some of the ideas that add sight or sound to a story also add touch. Moving puppets of sheep or of people, for example, involves touching. Building the walls of Jericho or Noah's ark involves touch too.

Tip #3: Use the children's names in the story.

Have you noticed how your attention is drawn whenever someone says your name? Teachers can use this common response to regain children's attention during a story. There are several ways to work children's names into Bible stories. For example, while preparing a story stay alert to traits that your students have in common with Bible characters. You might say, "David loved to sing to God, just like Milta likes to sing in our class."

Also plan to use names when children get restless. While telling Bible stories, stay alert to children's body language. Body language can signal a child's need to be refocused on the Bible story. Suppose a child's attention begins to wander during a story just as Goliath sees David walking toward him. You might say, "*Jason*, what do you think Goliath's face looked like when he was angry?" Notice that the child's name begins the sentence. Using his name first draws the child's attention back to what you are saying. Then, asking the child to answer a question about the story or to participate in some way refocuses him on the story.

Tip #4: Focus on events of high interest to preschoolers.

When preparing to tell a Bible story, try to decide what event in that story will be the most interesting or the most memorable from a child's point of view. Children may focus on very different events than adults would. Consider the following stories as examples:

STORY	**FOCUS OF INTEREST FOR CHILD**
Baby Moses	Floating in a basket
Daniel	Being in a lions den
Noah	Working with the animals
Zaccheus	Climbing a tree
The Good Shepherd	Looking for the sheep

After deciding what part of a story will be of natural interest to preschoolers, plan ways to emphasize that part of the story. Why? The interest in and emphasis on the focal point will make the whole story more memorable to young children.

There are many ways to plan more emphasis for these focal points. For Baby Moses bring a wicker basket, doll, and blanket. Demonstrate how Moses' mother may have wrapped the baby and placed him in a basket. Or pour a couple inches of water in the bottom of a tub and show how a plastic bowl will float. Compare your display with the "basket boat" that held Moses.

Each Bible story will include events of interest to preschoolers. By placing extra emphasis on that part of the story, you will keep the children's attention and help them remember God's Word.

Tip #5: Emphasize God's part of the story.

It's important that children know you are telling stories from the Bible and that the stories are true. To many preschoolers, stories about the three bears or Mickey Mouse are just as "real" as stories about Esther or Jesus. As the children grow older, most will automatically begin to sort true events from imaginary tales. In the meantime, teachers can create Bible story routines that will help preschoolers begin to understand that the Bible tells how God helps real people.

If possible, equip your room with a number of Bibles. During stories give each child a Bible to hold. Emphasize that you are telling a story from the Bible. Stress that Bible stories are true.

Use your voice and facial expressions to emphasize the importance of God's parts in the Bible stories. Look very serious, for example, when you tell how Jonah tried to run away from God. Crease your forehead as you stage whisper, "Jonah thought that if he sailed on a ship, God could not find him. But God is everywhere!" On the other hand, after the Israelites cross the Red Sea safely, you might laugh and clap and maybe even ask the children to join you in dancing around the room like the Bible characters. By matching your face and voice to the emotion of God's part in Bible stories, you will convince children that you believe what the Bible says about God's mighty deeds. This use of your voice and face will also help keep the children's attention by building drama about what God will do next in the story.

Tip #6: Use the time just before and just after the story to focus children's attention on the story.

Just before each Bible story, use an activity that will focus the children's attention on the story. Before the story of the Good Shepherd, children could practice moving sheep puppets like the flock in the story. Before the story of Jesus' stilling the storm, children could sit around the edge of a bed sheet and pretend to make small and big waves. Another time, they could close their eyes like Blind Bartimaeus and use only their ears to identify recorded sounds. Any of these methods would create interest in the Bible story that you are about to tell.

After each Bible story, plan to use an activity that reviews or reinforces an important part of the story. After telling about the Good Shepherd, ask children to look for a lost toy sheep and to rejoice when it is found. After hearing about Jesus and the stormy sea, children could act out the story. Sometimes children could examine items related to some part of a story. After hearing about Bartimaeus, they could compare Braille books and picture books and thank God for eyes that see. Any of these methods would reinforce the message of the Bible story.

COMBINE TECHNIQUES IN EVERY STORY

While planning how to tell each Bible story, expect to combine several of the storytelling techniques to draw preschooler's attention back to the story. Let's plan how to combine techniques to tell the story of Mary and Joseph fleeing to Egypt.

TELLING TECHNIQUE	**USE IN THIS STORY**
Pre-Story Activity	Before the story the teacher can prepare a doll for bed.
Active Involvement	When describing Jesus' family preparing for bed, the teacher can ask all children to stretch, yawn, and pretend to spread blankets over themselves.
Sense: Sight	She can display a visual of an angel.
Use Names	The teacher can ask a specific child if he has ever dreamed about an angel.
Emphasize God's Part	In a soft voice the teacher can explain how God sent the angel to warn Joseph of danger.
Active Involvement	All children can pretend to wake up and pretend to pack.
Sense: Sight	The teacher can display a visual of Joseph, Mary, and Baby Jesus starting the trip.
Sense: Hearing	All children can make the sounds of walking on a trip.
Active Involvement	All children raise hands to thank God for His protection.

Each time the teacher shows a visual, calls a name, or involves the children in an action, she uses an effective storytelling technique to draw attention back to the Bible story. The frequent engagement of the preschoolers' attention not only extends the amount of time to tell the Bible story but also increases the amount of the story the children will remember.

JESUS TOLD STORIES

When Jesus lived on earth, He frequently used stories to teach about the Kingdom of God. I like to imagine Jesus sitting on a boulder. A large crowd of adults and children are scattered on the hillside around Jesus. As Jesus begins to describe how well God can take care of us, a flock of chirping birds flies overhead. The birds draw the attention of some children and adults. So what does Jesus do? He points up at the birds and includes them in His teaching. "Look at the birds of the air," Jesus says. "They do not plant or harvest food, and yet God feeds them. God loves you more than many birds."

It's just in my imagination, of course, but I like to think that Jesus' listeners were sometimes distracted. But Jesus, the Master Storyteller, knew many techniques to regain their attention and help them remember the lessons that stories can teach about God.

Ministry Check:

Use this time to employ the telling techniques from this chapter.

Write the title of the Bible story you will tell next. _____

_____

As you prepare the Bible story, use the blanks to jot down at least one possible way to use each tip.

1. Involve the children actively in the story. _____

_____

2. Appeal to the children's five senses. _____

_____

3. Use the children's names in the story. _____

_____

4. Focus on events of high interest to children. _____

_____

5. Emphasize God's part of the story. _____

_____

6. Extend the story with before and after activities. _____

_____

Hands-On Learning For Every Child

12

I **can do** everything through him who gives
me strength (Philippians 4:13).

Questions to Answer:

1. How will a teacher's confidence in God's resourcefulness affect his or her attitude toward hands-on learning?

2. How can hands-on learning be used in small rooms? in big rooms?

3. If the teacher and students are used to a sit-and-listen model of learning, how should hands-on learning be introduced?

4. What learning supplies can be made, borrowed, or brought from home?

In Deuteronomy 6:7,8, God describes how He wants children to learn about Him. He says to give children spiritual training on-the-go—when they get up in the morning, when they sit down to eat, and as they go from place to place. The on-the-go model of learning that God describes fits the way God has designed children to learn—through their senses and through activity.

Often the Church follows a different model from the one in Deuteronomy. Instead of teaching children on-the-go, we attempt to teach children as if they were at public school—sitting quietly while they watch and listen to the teacher.

This public school model of training lends itself more to head knowledge than to heartfelt dependence on God.

Every teacher must decide which model to follow as he or she teaches young children. This chapter explains how to adapt the Deuteronomy model for learning at church as well as at home. In fact if teachers will use on-the-go learning at church, children are more likely to repeat those same activities at home.

ATTITUDE MAKES A DIFFERENCE

The teacher's attitude will affect which teaching style he or she chooses to use at Sunday school. I know this from personal experience. My attitude has changed over the years. The first Sunday school class I ever taught met in a tiny room. We didn't have wall-to-wall carpet, but we did have wall-to-wall table. The room was so small and the table took so much space that the children had to walk in single file in order to reach their chairs. When everyone was seated, there was room to close the door and set up the flannelboard. It was a tight fit.

While I taught in that tiny room, I had a "can't do" attitude about the Deuteronomy model of learning.

"I can't use hands-on learning—there's no room."

"I can't use hands-on learning—there are no toys."

"I can't use hands-on learning—there is no money to buy supplies."

At some point God changed my focus from what I can't do, to what I **can do** with God's help. In Philippians 4:13, the Bible tells us we **can do** all things because God will give us strength to do them. God wants to give His strength and resourcefulness to teachers.

Since God changed my attitude, I have thought about my first class in different terms. If I returned to that tiny classroom today, I would use hands-on learning with the children. With my confidence set on God, I would respond to limited resources differently. With God's help, I would say, "When I can't do what the quarterly suggests, **what can I do instead?**"

The quarterly suggests pretending to cook in the homeliving center. We don't have a homeliving center. But I **can** use a masking tape circle to make a pretend burner on the table in front of each child. I **can** bring pots and pans from home to set on the circles. I **can** help children cut out food pictures from old magazines. We **can** pretend to cook the pictures in the pans. We **can** glue food pictures to paper plates. I **can** use conversation to connect our pretend play with thanking God for our food.

Perhaps you wonder whether you're creative enough to make these kinds of lesson adaptations. Remember that where you feel weak you can depend on God's strength. God's Spirit is creative. If you ask Him, He will help you creatively substitute hands-on learning **YOU can do** for methods that won't work in your setting. Read the rest of this chapter asking the Holy Spirit to give you a "**CAN-do**" attitude about hands-on learning in your class.

MAKING A HANDS-ON INVENTORY

How much on-the-go, hands-on learning do you use in your class? The "Hands-On Checklist" in this chapter lists 20 methods preschool children can use to learn spiritual lessons. Read through the checklist. Count the methods your students already use at church to learn about God.

Hands-On Checklist

* *Asterisked items can be set up at a table or a learning center.*

___ lesson-related puzzles*	___ play dough activities*
___ action songs*	___ rhythm instruments*
___ marching & chants	___ picture books*
___ movement games	___ matching games*
___ coloring	___ painting*
___ drawing on chalkboard*	___ cutting & pasting*
___ climbing & sliding	___ acting out Bible story
___ pretending to be animals*	___ building with blocks*
___ drama with puppets*	___ sand activities*
___ drama with costumes	___ water activities*

Total methods used regularly in Bible lessons ___

STARTING WITH HANDS-ON LEARNING

If you and your children haven't used hands-on methods, plan to introduce this kind of on-the-go learning a little at a time. Both teacher and students will need time to adjust.

As the teacher, you will need time to learn how to organize hands-on activities in order to get the best cooperation from the children. You will also need time to gradually develop hands-on teaching skills, such as making puzzles, using puppets, or cooking play dough. Finally, you will need time to gradually accumulate, purchase, and/or recognize possible learning supplies and equipment. Your students also will need time to switch from sit-and-listen lessons to hands-on learning. Preschoolers need to learn routines for gluing, for using play dough, for moving from one activity to the next, and so on. Young children also need to learn that during some parts of each lesson they can choose what to do, but during other times they must do what the teacher says.

BEGINNING IN A SMALLER ROOM

If I were to return to my first classroom, I would use hands-on learning. I would begin by using one activity at a time; and because the room was small, I would need to plan tabletop activities. When the children finished with one activity, we would clear the table and set out supplies for the next. Of the 20 activities in the "Hands-On Checklist," all the asterisked (*) methods could be used while sitting at a table or standing just behind a chair. Many other methods can be adapted to a tabletop setting as well.

For the first few months, I would probably plan only two or three hands-on activities per lesson, and usually these activities would be variations on using play dough, dramatizing stories, putting together puzzles, and creating tabletop art. In the beginning, I would probably need to show children what routines to follow for each activity. As children became skilled at using play dough, gluing pictures, moving toy people in tabletop dramas, etc. I would begin with two activities at a time. This could be done by using tape to divide the table into two centers. Children would be able to choose how they learned. Making choices motivates children. Choosing between learning activities also allows them to match how they learn about the Bible with their personal learning style.

The same kinds of hands-on activities would continue, but now two at a time rather than one after another. On one Sunday, for example, children at one end of the table could use water colors to paint pictures of the river where Baby Moses floated. Children at the other end could shape play dough into little baskets. While standing near the table, I could still show how to use materials, help children share supplies, draw attention to good work, help children trade places as they finish each project, and use conversation to connect both activities with the Bible lesson about Moses. Eventually, several hands-on methods could be used at the table at the same time.

BEGINNING IN A LARGER ROOM

In a larger room, children and teacher have freedom to use even more kinds of on-the-go Bible learning. Even with more space, if only one teacher works with the class, it is better to introduce hands-on learning a little at a time. Children will need to learn how to do the activities. The teacher will need to decide where to do different activities. The teacher will also need to train students to use different centers in specific ways. All this can be done with less confusion one activity at a time.

During the first several months of using hands-on learning, the teacher should arrive early enough to pray and to set up learning activities in various parts of the room. When the first child arrives, the teacher will begin one hands-on learning activity. As other students come, the teacher can invite them to join the activity already in progress. When most of the children are finished with the first activity, the group can move to the location of activity two. Teachers can encourage children to clean up each area before moving to the next activity.

When more than one teacher works with a class, several kinds of hands-on learning can be active at the same time. With this option, every teacher will be in charge of one activity. If three teachers work together, children choose from two or three activities at a time.

Choosing Specific Methods

There are hundreds of different methods teachers can use for hands-on learning at church. Teachers can find hands-on idea books in libraries, bookstores, and education catalogs. To help teachers get started with the Deuteronomy model of hands-on learning, this chapter will describe a few methods involving play dough, drama, and art activities.

How To Teach With Play Dough

Preschoolers of all ages enjoy play dough and will interact with it at their own level of ability. Even after using play dough for a month of Sundays, children will return to class eager to use it again.

Homemade Play Dough

The least expensive play dough is homemade. Homemade dough feels softer than commercial Play-Doh, and is easier to shape and reshape. Play dough is easy to make; and, since it's made from flour and salt, it is nontoxic to preschoolers who often taste what their fingers get into. Since preschoolers could choke on play dough, a teacher should always supervise its use. If you have never made play dough, try my favorite recipe. In a medium sauce pan, mix:

    2 cups flour   2 cups water
    1 cup salt   2 tablespoons oil
    4 teaspoons cream of tartar
    1 package unsweetened fruit-flavored drink mix

Mix in a medium pan. At first, the mixture will look like a lumpy soup. Cook over medium heat, stirring with a large spoon. As dough forms, use the spoon to turn and knead the dough. Check for doneness by pressing shallow dents in dough with your finger. If the dough feels sticky, cook it longer. Cool and store in a plastic bag or airtight container. This recipe makes enough dough for six to eight children.

Play Dough Activities

You will probably find many ways to relate play dough to Bible lessons, but here are 19 suggestions to get started.

Bible Story Activities

1. Cut animal shapes to lay in a cardboard "ark" or "stable."
2. Use free-form "stones" from all children to build one sheepfold for the Good Shepherd's sheep.
3. Stockpile play dough loaves in a tabletop barn with Joseph.
4. Lay small pieces of play dough all over a tabletop like manna. Collect manna in play dough baskets.

Cooperation Activities

1. Ask each child to use his cookie cutter to make a part of a scene, such as flowers and animals in a garden.
2. Work in teams to make families of various sizes. (Include animal families.)
3. Give each child a paper plate and ask him to choose a kind of food to shape (e.g., corn, chicken, grapes). Each child should shape enough of his food to put on everyone's plate.
4. Before retelling a Bible story, assign each child a background shape or person to make (e.g., stars,

ladder, angels, and a man for the story of Jacob's ladder).

5. Make I-do-you-do shapes. For example, one part at a time, form the body, fins, and eyes of a fish. Ask each child to watch what you do and imitate your model.

Sharing Activities

1. Ask for help to pass out play dough and/or cookie cutters. Tell helpers that God sees them sharing.

2. Help each child pull a bit of play dough from his portion to give to a latecomer. Show appreciation for the way the children shared with their friend.

3. Give each child a mound of dough and a plastic knife. Let each child cut off pieces of his "loaf" to give to others at the table.

4. Give each child a cookie cutter, perhaps one that represents a part of creation. Ask the child to make enough copies of his shape to share with others.

5. Encourage children to count play dough shapes and to make sure everyone has an equal number.

Miscellaneous Activities

1. Use a mound of play dough as the base for a group silk-flower arrangement. (Cut the stem of each flower to be only 2 to 3 inches long).

2. Press coins, seashells, old jewelry, etc., into play dough to make interesting designs.

3. Use plastic knives to cut out play dough shapes of children's hands. Count the hands God made.

4. Squeeze play dough through a garlic press to make grass, hair, or decorations for pretend cookies.

5. Let children push birthday candles into a lump of dough to decorate a birthday cake for Baby Jesus or for children in the room. Sing "Happy Birthday."

HOW TO TEACH WITH DRAMA

Drama brings Bible stories to life. When children just listen to Bible stories, they learn *about* God's people. When children dramatize Bible stories, they *"become"* God's people in action. Through drama children can also identify how God's people felt during Bible events.

Life application dramas help children experiment with responses to everyday events. With teacher guidance they can begin to decide which pretend responses would please God if used in real life. Many preschoolers are good at life application drama because their pretend play is an early childhood version of drama.

Stages of Early Childhood Drama

Students' ages influence how they participate in dramas. For toddlers, drama takes the form of imitating specific actions or expressions. A 1-year-old will act out jabbering on a pretend phone, for instance, or imitate his teacher's sad expression just for fun. The same child can also imitate the way his teacher moves a stick puppet or toy car in a drama.

By the time children are 2½ years old, many can use imitation to act out whole stories. At this age, however, all the children want to be all the characters. So, in a drama of Jonah, everyone plays the part of Jonah.

Preschoolers who are 3, 4, and 5 years old are ready to begin using drama in more expected ways. Everyone will still want to participate, but teachers can ask for volunteers to play various roles. As teachers describe story actions, the children will be able to act out their characters' responses.

Drama Activities

When a budget is available, churches can purchase or make real costumes, props, and puppets to use in dramas. (See "Equipment" in Chapter 9 for addresses of companies that sell these kinds of props for dramatic play.) Purchased extras can add to the realism of dramas, but they are not necessary. Preschoolers will happily use their imaginations to turn everyday items into accessories for a drama. A bed sheet can become clothing for an angel, a tent for Abraham, the wall of Jericho, or a sea on which to sail. The following ideas suggest specific ways to encourage preschoolers to use their imaginations in lesson-related dramas.

Drama With Art

1. Cut out paper fish silhouettes. Let the children color in details of eyes, scales, and fins to use in acting out a story.
2. Glue food pictures to paper plates to serve during a life application set in a restaurant or home.
3. Provide a large sheet of white paper. Ask children to draw the Garden of Gethsemane to use as a backdrop for acting out the Easter story.
4. Trace or photocopy a coloring picture onto an overhead transparency. Project the picture onto a large piece of white paper. Retrace the picture to make a large camel for the Wise Men, a huge elephant for the ark, a big lion for Samson, or a stable for Baby Jesus. Let the children work together to color the big picture before performing the drama.

Drama With Costumes

1. Bring shirts and towels from home to use in biblical dramas. (Sew elastic into headbands and slip them over the tops of towels to hold headdresses in place.)
2. Purchase patterns for biblical costumes from McCall's or Simplicity. Ask a church member or the women's group to make costumes for the class. Combine these costumes in various ways to act out many Bible stories.
3. Purchase or draw masks to use in dramas.
4. Draw the bodies or clothes of characters on poster board. Ask children to hold these "costumes" just below their chins as they act out the drama.

Drama With Props

1. Provide several flashlights and lunch-size paper bags to use as torches and pottery in acting out the story of Gideon's army.

2. Ask each child to bring a stuffed animal to class to use in acting out naming animals in the Garden of Eden.

3. Rearrange classroom chairs to use in various Bible dramas (e.g., the shape of Noah's ark, the walls of Jericho, seats on a church bus, or sofas and beds).

Drama in Interest Centers

1. Homeliving: Change the accessories in the area from time to time to create a new setting for dramas, such as shops, restaurants, hospitals, and laundromats.

2. Block: Use tape to outline the shape of a boat, house, tower, or road. Lay blocks along the tape outline to build a prop to use in a drama.

3. Large Muscle: Pretend climbing equipment is a prison for Paul, a house for Peter, or a mountain for Moses.

4. Music: Act out songs that tell stories about Bible characters, such as Zaccheus, Father Abraham, Noah, and David. Make up new songs to familiar tunes to go with other Bible stories. Be sure the new words describe actions the children can do dramatically.

Drama in Small Rooms

If you minister in a small room, you can still teach with drama. Perform mini-dramas on the tabletop with toy people and small props. For example, give each child some kind of toy person (e.g., a Lego figure, a clothespin doll, or a story visual glued to poster board). As you describe a Bible story, ask the children to move their people on the tabletop to match the plot. In the story of the Red Sea, for example, ask two children to lay two blue towels on the table to represent the sea. Another child could move a posterboard cloud between the toys representing God's people and those of Egyptian characters. Then children could pull apart the two towels to represent the parting of the Red Sea. Everyone could move God's people through the sea. When the Egyptians try to cross, however, the children can cover them with the towels. Then children could move the toys that represent God's people as if jumping and dancing to celebrate God's rescue.

Some tabletop dramas won't even require props. The children can walk their fingers along the tabletop, or pound the table to sound like marching soldiers or running feet. Even while seated in their chairs, children can pretend to be on a racing chariot. As the teacher dramatizes the story with gestures and facial expressions, children will be happy to imitate her actions.

HOW TO TEACH WITH ART

Coloring with crayons is perhaps the most commonly used hands-on activity in Sunday school. Even though it's easy to allow children to color a lesson-related picture, teachers still need to adapt even coloring to different preschool abilities. At first, teachers may need to tape toddlers' papers to the table to help hold the papers still while 1-year-olds color. As they grow older, children learn to hold the pictures themselves.

Children's first attempts at art are "scribble coloring." Some children will be finished after making only one or two scribbles. Others will energetically scribble on both sides of the paper. Your positive comments about "scribble coloring" build children's confidence in their abilities. As children grow older, coloring skills improve. Even so, some children will want to color faces green and hair purple. Allow this expression of creativity.

Most children enjoy coloring at first. After a while, however, children grow bored with coloring. Other art activities can be added to renew interest and reinforce learning.

Finding Art Supplies

As with play dough, art supplies can be modified to fit any budget. When funds are available, teachers can purchase paints, easels, brushes, art papers, and kits from catalog companies or school supply stores. When funds are scarce, teachers can still offer a variety of art activities that use available supplies like wallpaper samples; grocery bags; magazine pictures; used greeting cards and wrapping paper; scraps of fabric, yarn, and ribbon; inexpensive sponges; colored pasta, rice, or salt; or seeds, sand, and pebbles. Many such supplies are readily at hand in many homes. Alert teachers will set aside such items to use in art activities at church.

Homemade Watercolor Paints

Painting is a nice alternative to crayons. A teacher from New York, shared the following inexpensive way to make watercolor paints. For each color, cut a thin sponge to fit in the bottom of a baby food jar. Add 15 to 20 drops of food coloring to the sponge. Moisten the sponge enough to be damp without forming a puddle in the jar. Press a watercolor paint brush against the sponge to mix the color and water. Between Sundays, store the watercolor paint jars without lids. They will dry out, but not mildew. The next time the paints are needed, just add water to the sponges. When the color begins to fade, add a few more drops of food coloring.

Before children paint, always cover their clothing with paint smocks or old shirts worn backwards. Children can paint at a table or an easel. Painting at an easel keeps children's arms from resting on wet paint. So, before children paint at a table, roll up any long sleeves, and ask children to stand while they paint in order to keep paint off their arms.

Painting Activities

1. Children paint the picture on take-home papers.

2. Children work together to paint a BIG picture enlarged with an overhead projector.

3. Children paint pictures of items related to a Bible story (e.g., plants before and after a drought, fish from the boy's lunch, animals at the manger).

4. Children paint details on paper cutouts related to the lesson (e.g., a pitcher for Rebekah or a coat for Joseph).

5. Rather than using a brush, children can paint colorful designs with sponges, potato mashers, eye droppers, etc. After the designs dry, use them for wrapping paper or as backgrounds for printed Bible verses.

Gluing

Children enjoy the "magic" of making one item stick to another. Art that children glue can be sent home as lesson reminders. Don't be surprised, however, if preschoolers seem to forget about art projects as soon as they finish working. During the preschool years, the *process* of doing the art is much more enjoyable to the children than the finished *product*. Even so, gluing provides interesting ways to reinforce Bible learning. A montage can include many parts of creation. Puppets children make can be used to tell the Bible story.

Gluing With Less Mess

Gluing can be messy for young children, but it doesn't have to be. Organizing the gluing projects is a key to reducing untidiness. When setting out supplies for a gluing project, save the glue for last. When all other supplies have been distributed, give each child a cotton swab to use as a glue spreader. Then pour a quarter-sized dab of glue on a paper plate or in a small paper cup. Show how to use the swab to spread glue on the project. If a child runs low on glue, give him another dab. If a cotton swab becomes too messy, replace it. This controlled approach to gluing, reduces messiness. Also provide damp paper towels or wet wipes to wipe sticky fingers and tables after the project.

Gluing Activities

1. Prepare go-anywhere gluing projects for younger children (e.g., stars on blue paper, sheep in a pasture, food photos on a paper plate.)

2. Cut out magazine pictures for children to glue on a lesson-related montage (e.g., people God loves, ways we travel to church, food we thank God for).

3. Add texture to pictures. (With sand, salt, or rice, children can spread glue on the picture then turn the picture, sticky-side down, in a pan of the texturing material. With flat textures like fabric, children can spread glue on either surface. With 3-dimensional textures like pasta or pebbles, children can dip the texturing item in glue and then press it on the picture.)

4. Cut out shapes for the children to assemble and glue to a background (e.g., a triangle and square positioned to look like a house; eyes, mouth, and nose to go on a face; petals to fit on the stem of a flower.)

5. Show children how to glue strips of paper into an interlocking chain. Work on the project as a group to make a very long chain.

EQUIPPING FOR HANDS-ON LEARNING

It should be clear that hands-on learning fits any budget, since many readily available items can be used in hands-on learning.

■ Learning supplies can be carried from home or borrowed and returned (e.g., a satchel to pack for a Bible trip, a plastic tub to use in water play).

■ Students can bring items that will fit a particular lesson (e.g., a piece of fruit or a toy vehicle).

■ Learning supplies can be created from common items (e.g., plastic cups as cookie cutters, or metal spoons and unsharpened pencils as rhythm instruments).

As funds become available, it's good to begin to purchase permanent learning supplies and equipment, such as a play kitchen stove, an indoor slide, a set of blocks, etc. Some parents may be willing to help purchase such items. Other parents will watch garage sales for second-hand equipment that is durable enough for group learning. Still others may be willing to donate toys and equipment as their children outgrow them. Share with the pastor your vision of Christian education for everyday living. Prepare a budget request for the pastor and the board. They may say no, but they could say yes.

Whether you are able to obtain a budget or not, remember that money is not your main ministry resource—God is. God will give you the resourcefulness you need to nurture faith in the lives of your young students.

Ministry Check:

If you want to use more hands-on learning in your teaching ministry, the following checklist will help you decide what steps to take next. As you review the list, check methods and resources you already employ. Then decide which unchecked items you can begin adding to your ministry.

__ Lessons include at least three hands-on activities, used one after another.

__ Lessons include several tabletop hands-on learning activities.

__ Lessons include several kinds of on-the-go learning that occur simultaneously in different parts of the room.

__ Children know what activities occur in different areas of the room.

__ Children know routines for using play dough, paint, glue, and other hands-on resources.

__ Helpers know how to connect activities to lesson objectives.

__ Teacher brings learning supplies from home.

__ Children bring learning supplies from home.

__ Parents help provide learning supplies.

__ Church budget pays for learning supplies.

Team Teaching With Parents

13

[God] wants everyone to change his heart and life (2 Peter 3:9, *International Children's Bible*).

Questions To Answer:

1. *How many children out of 100 will probably become Christians while preschoolers?*

2. *How does God intend parents to promote spiritual growth in their children?*

3. *How can parents and teachers team up to disciple children?*

How old were you when God changed your heart and life—when you became a Christian? According to one resource, 85% of all conversions occur between the ages of 5 and 14. Do you fit in that category? How many of your students are likely to become Christians during their preschool years? According to the same source, only 1% of all conversions occur at or before the age of 4.

AUBREY JOINS THE KINGDOM

Aubrey fits into the 1%. She became a Christian when she was 3 years old. Aubrey and her little sister Stephany had attended church since they were infants. Both their parents were Christians who not only brought their girls to church regularly but who also taught their daughters about God at home.

One day while Aubrey and Stephany rode in their car seats, their mother heard 2-year-old Stephi ask Aubrey, "Do you know that Jesus died on the cross?"

"Yes," said Aubrey, "But the best part of that story is that Jesus came back to life." At that point Aubrey turned to her mother and said, "Mommy, Jesus' disciples called Him *master*. What is a *master*?"

The mother, who had been driving and listening, carefully responded to Aubrey's question. She explained, as simply as she could, that the disciples called Jesus master because Jesus was their leader. The disciples loved and obeyed Jesus.

After listening and thinking, Aubrey asked, "Can Jesus be my master too?" That day Aubrey's mother had the joy of leading her daughter to Christ.

Aubrey's decision to ask Jesus to be her master came after receiving 3 years of Bible teaching both at Sunday school and at home. Stephany did not ask Jesus to be her master that day. At 2, she was not ready for a genuine salvation experience. Yet, Stephi was the one who began the conversation about Jesus. In her everyday thinking, Stephi included thoughts about God's Son right along with thoughts about playing, eating, and sleeping.

Stephi and Aubrey are good examples of what can happen in the lives of very young children when their church and their parents team up to introduce them to God.

GOD'S COMMAND TO PARENTS

Throughout the Bible, parents carry the main responsibility for children's spiritual growth. Scripture describes various ways parents can teach about God.

From generation to generation, Christian parents tell children about God's presence in their own lives. I can imagine Old Testament parents telling children about their encounters with God. Abraham probably told Isaac about the miracle of Isaac's birth. I imagine Isaac and Rebekah told Esau and Jacob how God used camels and water to start their family. Jacob must have told Joseph about his dream of the ladder reaching to heaven. Each generation of God's people have personal experiences with God that they can tell their children.

In addition to personal experiences, Psalm 78 lists Bible stories parents are to tell their children so each generation will "put their trust in God and . . . keep his commands" (verse 7). The stories are the same ones told in Sunday school—the dividing of the Red Sea, being guided by the cloud and fire, and eating manna in the wilderness. Deuteronomy 6:5-7, also directs parents to teach God's commands to children: "Talk about them when you sit at home and when you walk along the road, when you lie down and when you get up."

In Proverbs 22:6 God tells parents to train their young children well so they will follow God's ways even as adults.

THE BENEFITS OF TEAMWORK

Quite often in today's world, however, many parents depend on the church to prepare their preschoolers for salvation. Yet, children are in church only a few hours per week. Young children benefit spiritually when parents and church teachers cooperate at church and at home to help children love, trust, and obey God. The Bible story that is taught at God's house on Sunday can be repeated with drama at the child's house on Tuesday. A pumpkin seed the child planted in Sunday school can be watered and watched at home during the week. A stuffed animal a child loves at home can be carried to church to place in Noah's ark on Sunday. The transfer of stories, projects, and toys between home and church extends faith building and Bible learning for children. They receive spiritual training daily.

LAY THE GROUNDWORK FOR TEAMWORK

Many sports are played in teams. Successful teams have mastered teamwork. Sports teams do not just happen—they are carefully built. Churches who want to benefit children's spiritual growth by teaming up with parents also need to begin building teams. If this process is to begin, church teachers will usually be the ones to take the first steps. Read the following team-building ideas. Decide how far the process has already come in your Sunday school.

Be a Communicator With Parents

When a child arrives or leaves your class, try to take a little time to talk with his parents. Since your main task is to teach and care for the children, you may not have time to greet every parent every week. Do, however, make an effort to talk with two or three different parents every week. Focus at least part of this conversation on their children's feats, activities, or friendships in class. In order to have this kind of information to tell parents, try to watch for specific positive events that can be shared. If there is no time to talk in this way at church, try to phone one or two parents during the week. When you call, parents will know you are thinking about their children during the week. They will know that you take your ministry to their children seriously.

Photographs can also help build teamwork with parents. Occasionally, photograph your students while they learn Bible lessons in your class. Give these photos to parents as a visual record of their children's experiences at church. On the back of each photo, write a brief description of the Bible learning shown. Encourage the parents to use the photos to talk with their children about what they like to learn at church.

The U.S. Postal Service can help you begin to team teach with parents. All children love to receive mail. So send postcards about Bible lessons to the children. Since preschoolers can't read, parents will read your messages aloud to them—the parents will get the message too. Also use cards to announce upcoming events. As the teacher makes an effort to share a child's church experiences with the parents, they will come to understand that the teacher is investing herself in their child's spiritual well-being. Most parents will respect teachers for that and will be more willing to team up with the teacher to minister to their children.

Be a Supporter of Parents

Most parents receive more training to drive their cars than to rear their children. In fact most adults have learned how to be parents by watching our own parents. What happens, though, if a couples' parents had very different parenting styles? Which parenting style will the young parents choose? What if one set of parents were abusive? What if one set were not Christians? What happens if a young father was raised without a father to imitate? Churches can team up with young parents to help them nurture children to love, trust, and obey God.

Churches can lend ministry resources to parents to use at home. Examples of resources that can help parents train young children spiritually are Bible story videos, Christian music videos or audio recordings, Christian picture books, and preschool devotional activity books. It's possible that parents would even be willing to help the church purchase these kinds of resources for all church families to share. Once parents find Christian songs and stories that their children enjoy, they will probably decide to buy personal copies.

Churches can also support parents by creating or by passing out Christian parenting newsletters. *Radiant Life* early childhood curriculum includes three take-home papers for parents.

Parenting Helps is a monthly take-home paper for the parents of babies, toddlers, and twos. Each issue includes articles about practical and spiritual parenting ideas and at-home activities related to weekly Sunday school lessons.

Preschool Parenting and *Kindergarten Parenting* are the parent papers that automatically come with *Radiant Life* take-home papers for older preschoolers. Articles describe Christian parenting. Questions and answers deal with common parenting issues. One section offers at-home activities that extend each Sunday school lesson.

Check at your local Christian bookstore for other parenting resources that can support young parents as they begin to disciple their little ones.

Christian bookstores offer many books, tapes, and videos that deal with Christian parenting. Churches can purchase some of these resources to lend to parents who attend with their children.

Be a Seeker of Unsaved Parents

According to one *USA Today* poll, 40% of all American adults attend church more regularly after becoming parents. Some of these adults were raised in the church but stopped attending after high school. Often these young adults stay out of church until the birth of their first child. When that baby is born, many adults turn to the church for help. New parents who begin attending church are wanting help in two areas. They want to give their child a good start in learning how to live, and they want to know how to be the best parents possible.

Churches can use the first years of parenting, when young adults are open to advice, to minister to parents and babies. Churches can choose from a number of ministry options. They can send a Little Lamb cradle roll congratulations card to new parents (available from Gospel Publishing House, 1445 Boonville, Springfield, MO 65802). They can visit parents in the hospital and give rose buds or small baby gifts. Church members can prepare meals and deliver them when a baby comes home from the hospital. Churches can sponsor parenting support groups, seminars, or Sunday school electives about Christian parenting. They can ask church parents to follow up young parents who visit the church. (Young parents will have common interests and questions to build relationships on.) Churches can recruit experienced Christian parents who have grown Christian children to listen to and support new parents who are just getting started.

Each of the ministry options provides a meaningful way for churches to draw in parents who are not Christians and seek to bring them to a saving relationship with Jesus.

TEAM UP AT CHURCH

Parents and teachers can team up in Sunday school to support one another in ministry to children. Parents can support Sunday schools by becoming rotating helpers in early childhood classes. Sunday schools can support parents by teaching Bible lessons in ways that parent helpers can imitate with their children during the week—at breakfast, in the car, and all around the house. When young parents work with master teachers, they may actually receive indirect training in disciplining and discipling their children lovingly and appropriately. Most of each month, young parents can use their time at church to worship, to receive ministry, and to fellowship with Christian adults, but once a month parents can help minister to their children.

Create a Team Vision

Many churches have established a policy of "cooperative Christian education." In these churches every parent who brings a preschooler helps in one of the early childhood classes on a rotating basis. Often that means each parent works in an early childhood class once a month. One or more regular teachers also minister in each class. When parents minister, they assist the regular teachers.

Being sensitive to the relationships between parents and children is an important part of making this kind of system successful. Some parents can minister effectively in their own child's class. Others need to be assigned to a different class. Usually this decision is based on how the child acts when his parent is helping. Some children cannot share their parents; they want their parents' total attention. In such a case, the church can schedule the parent to help in a different early childhood class.

A few parents may already be ministering in the church many hours each week. Some of these busy parents will still want to participate in their children's Christian education. A few parents, however, will ask to be excused. If their other ministry takes 4 or more hours of a parent's time each week, honor such a request. In most cases, however, by explaining how their child will benefit, teachers can convince many parents that their time is needed in both ministries.

Request Parents' Help

If parents are not currently helping in your preschool ministry, you may need to create a vision for teaming parents with the church ministry to their children. Many parents expect to take their preschoolers to Sunday school and then leave for their own classes. If this is your situation, the first step to becoming a ministry team is to communicate how the team will function.

1. Let parents know why their help is needed.
2. Tell parents how often they will be asked to help.
3. Explain some ways parents will help.
4. Describe how Sunday school experiences can be extended into weekly living.

Ask for Information

It's possible that parents in your church have special abilities they could use in early childhood classes. Learn more about parents by asking them to fill out a parent ministry form. Once you know how parents are willing and able to help, begin to use their help as soon as possible.

Provide a Ministry Schedule

Someone will need to create a schedule that shows when and where each parent is scheduled to help. Below is a sample schedule for one week. The format will depend on the size of your church. The sample can be expanded or simplified as needed. Once the schedule is printed, post it where teachers and parents can refer to it. If possible, give copies of the schedule to each parent. If a parent cannot be present when he is scheduled to help, ask him to change places with another parent on the list.

KINDERGARTEN MINISTRY SCHEDULE			
FEB. 7 **SUNDAY SCHOOL**	**AM CHURCH**	**SUNDAY PM**	**WEDNESDAY**
1. Bronte Hunter	1. Kathy Strand	1. C.J. Cho	1. Jo Gray
2. Sharon Carter	2. Glen Ashley	2. Jenny Ball	2. Jenny Ball
3. Adam Mayer	3. Julie Gomez	3. Carie Day	3. Carie Drake

PARENT MINISTRY FORM

Our church wants to team up with parents to minister to young children. Please fill in the information below. We will use your information to help minister to all our children.

Name _____ **Date** _____

Home Address _____ **Phone** _____

My Child(ren)'s Name(s) & Age(s) _____

1. I prefer to help: _____ in my child's class; _____ not in my child's class; _____ I have no preference.

2. I would be able to help at any of the following services: _____ Sunday school; _____ Sunday morning; _____ Sunday evening; _____ Wednesday evening.

3. All parents work as classroom helpers. Occasionally, parents also help with other ministry projects. Please check ministry options you would be willing to try.

___ play instrument	___ assist teacher
___ lead songs in class	___ teach a class
___ punch out handwork	___ teach BGMC
___ prepare crafts	___ send greeting cards
___ make play dough	___ help with parties
___ keep records	___ photograph events
___ do secretarial tasks	___ collect picture books
___ prepare parent letters	___ start a picture file
___ help organize room	___ decorate bulletin boards
___ teach with puppets	___ organize outings
___ tell stories	___ help build projects
___ read books aloud	___ help with painting
___ lead games	___ sew dress-up clothes
___ bring a snack	___ pray for children

Provide Ministry Reminders

Parents who help once a month will probably need a reminder during the week before they work. Decide whether to make reminders by phone or by mail. If a call is made, use the time for relationship building. Many people who come to church hope to make Christian friends there. Phone calls can become relaxed times to visit as well as to remind them of ministry. Express appreciation for their help. Ask for feedback about their experience in the preschool area.

Postcards also make good reminders. Develop a routine message to send to all workers. The boxed copy gives one sample of a reminder card. While this kind of reminder doesn't allow relationship building, it takes less time.

❤ *Ministry Reminder* ❤

Thank you for teaming with our church to disciple young children. Your next ministry time is _____ on
(service time)
_____. If you cannot minister at that time,
(date)
please trade times with another member of the ministry team. *(Phone numbers are on the printed list.)*

May God bless your ministry to His little ones.

Thank you again,

_____
(my phone number)

❤ ● ❤ ● ❤ ● ❤ ● ❤ ● ❤ ● ❤

Whatever you did for one of the least of these brothers of mine, you did for me. Matthew 25:40

Say Thank You

Let parents know that you enjoy teaming with them to nurture their children. Occasionally, send a thank you card and note. Print a list of names of helpers in the church bulletin. Describe how helpful their presence is to you as well as to the children. One of the best ways to show real appreciation is to invite parents to make suggestions about how to improve the Sunday school. You can invite these comments either when you call to remind parents they are scheduled to help or in thank you notes or letters.

GIVE FAITH TIME TO GROW

When we minister to young children and their parents at church, we are planting seeds of faith. How quickly do we expect to see mature fruit-bearing faith? No farmer plants seed one day and returns the very next day expecting to gather a harvest. All seed takes time to grow. As adults faithfully teach Bible lessons to children, the Holy Spirit will be faithful to do his work too.

Ministry Check:

Use the following list to evaluate how much teamwork your church has with parents. Check one response for each item. Ask Sunday school leaders to help begin one or more ways to involve parents in ministry to their children.

BUILDING TEAMWORK	WE DO	WE COULD	WE WILL
COMMUNICATE WITH PARENTS			
Greet parents	____	____	____
Enroll newcomers	____	____	____
Describe activities	____	____	____
Phone during week	____	____	____
Mail announcements	____	____	____
Photograph students	____	____	____
SUPPORT PARENTS			
Lend story videos	____	____	____
Lend picture books	____	____	____
Lend music tapes	____	____	____

	WE DO	WE COULD	WE WILL
Give *Parenting Helps**	———	———	———
Preschool Parenting*	———	———	———
Lend parenting videos	———	———	———
Lend parenting books	———	———	———

SEEK UNCHURCHED PARENTS

Use cradle roll	———	———	———
Visit maternity wards	———	———	———
Prepare meals	———	———	———
Parenting seminars	———	———	———
Parenting electives	———	———	———
Parent mentors	———	———	———

TEACH WITH Parents

Create a shared vision	———	———	———
Describe class tasks	———	———	———
Gather information	———	———	———
Print a schedule	———	———	———
Send reminders	———	———	———
Show appreciation	———	———	———
Accept suggestions	———	———	———